Lowe's Home Plans

Small & Stylish
HOMES FROM 864 - 2,806 SQ. FT.

Home Plans - Small & Stylish Home Plans - This book is a collection of best-selling small and stylish plans from some of the nation's leading designers and architects. Only quality plans with sound design, functional layout, energy efficiency and affordability have been selected.

These plans cover a wide range of architectural styles in a popular range of sizes. A broad assortment is presented to match a wide variety of lifestyles and budgets. Each design page features floor plans, a front view of the house, and a list of special features. All floor plans show room dimensions, exterior dimensions and the interior square footage of the home.

Technical Specifications - At the time the construction drawings were prepared, every effort was made to ensure that these plans and specifications meet nationally recognized building codes (BOCA, Southern Building Code Congress and others). Because national building codes change or vary from area to area some drawing modifications and/or the assistance of a professional designer or architect may be necessary to comply with your local codes or to accommodate specific building site conditions. We advise you to consult with your local building official for information regarding codes governing your area.

Blueprint Ordering - Fast and Easy - Your ordering is made simple by following the instructions on page 288. See page 287 for more information on which types of blueprint packages are available and how many plan sets to order.

Your Home, Your Way - The blueprints you receive are a master plan for building your new home. They start you on your way to what may well be the most rewarding experience of your life.

House shown on front cover is Plan #532-072D-0001 and is featured on page 134.

Lowe's Small & Stylish Home Plans is published by HDA, Inc. (Home Design Alternatives), 944 Anglum Road, St. Louis, MO 63042. All rights reserved. Reproduction in whole or in part without written permission of the publisher is prohibited. Printed in U.S.A © 2004. Artist drawings and photos shown in this publication may vary slightly from the actual working drawings. Some photos are shown in mirror reverse. Please refer to the floor plan for accurate layout.

CONTENTS

Extras Available With The Lowe's Signature Series Home Plans 2

Quick And Easy Customizing 3

Paint-By-Number Wall Murals 4

Lowe's Signature Series Home Plans 5-128

Designer Series Home Plans 129-283

Our Blueprint Packages Offer 284

Other Helpful Building Aids 285

Home Plans Index 286-287

What Kind Of Plan Package Do You Need? 287

To Order Home Plans 288

Signature SERIES

HDA is proud to bring you this unprecedented offer of our Lowe's Signature Series featuring our most popular small and stylish plans. Never before has there been a compilation of home plans as you will find in this publication.

Home plans included in the Lowe's Signature Series are indicated by the Lowe's Signature Series logo shown above and are found on pages 5 through 128. The series is a special collection of our most popular and unique plans. This is the ideal place to begin your search for a new home. Browse the plans in the Lowe's Signature Series collection to discover a home with the options and special characteristics you need.

One of the main reasons for purchasing home plans from a publications such as this is to save you time and money. And, you will discover the extra benefits of the unique services offered through our Lowe's Signature Series of home plans.

Besides providing the expected beauty and functional efficiency of all our home plans, the Lowe's Signature Series offers detailed material lists unmatched in the industry today.

Material Lists

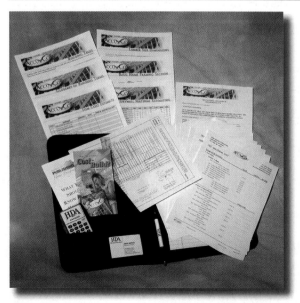

An accurate and detailed material list can save you a considerable amount of time and money. Our material lists give you the quantity, dimensions and descriptions of the major building materials necessary to construct your home. You'll get faster and more accurate bids from contractors and material suppliers, and you'll save money by paying for only the materials you need. Our package includes the material list, residential building resources, architect's scale, handy calculator, and convenient pen and paper all wrapped neatly in a durable leather portfolio. For availability and more information see the Index on page 286 and the Order Form on page 288.

Quick & Easy Customizing
Make Changes To Your Home Plan In 4 Steps

Here's an affordable and efficient way to make changes to your plan.

1. Select the house plan that most closely meets your needs. Purchase of a reproducible master is necessary in order to make changes to a plan.

2. Call 1-800-373-2646 or e-mail customize@hdainc.com to place your order. Tell the sales representative you're interested in customizing a plan. A $50 nonrefundable consultation fee will be charged. You will then be instructed to complete a customization checklist indicating all the changes you wish to make to your plan. You may attach sketches if necessary. <u>If you proceed with the custom changes the $50 will be credited to the total amount charged.</u>

3. FAX the completed customization checklist to our design consultant. Within 24-48* business hours you will be provided with a written cost estimate to modify your plan. Our design consultant will contact you by phone if you wish to discuss any of your changes in greater detail.

4. Once you approve the estimate, a 75% retainer fee is collected and customization work gets underway. Preliminary drawings can usually be completed within 5-10* business days. Following approval of the preliminary drawings your design changes are completed within 5-10* business days. Your remaining 25% balance due is collected prior to shipment of your completed drawings. You will be shipped five sets of revised blueprints or a reproducible master, plus a customized materials list if required.

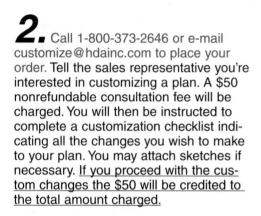

Before

After

Sample Modification Pricing Guide

The average prices specified below are provided as examples only. They refer to the most commonly requested changes, and are subject to change without notice. Prices for changes will vary or differ, from the prices below, depending on the number of modifications requested, the plan size, style, quality of original plan, format provided to us (originally drawn by hand or computer), and method of design used by the original designer. To obtain a detailed cost estimate or to get more information, please contact us.

Categories	Average Cost*
Adding or removing living space	Quote required
Adding or removing a garage	Starting at $400
Garage: Front entry to side load or vice versa	Starting at $300
Adding a screened porch	Starting at $280
Adding a bonus room in the attic	Starting at $450
Changing full basement to crawl space or vice versa	Starting at $495
Changing full basement to slab or vice versa	Starting at $495
Changing exterior building material	Starting at $200
Changing roof lines	Starting at $360
Adjusting ceiling height	Starting at $280
Adding, moving or removing an exterior opening	$65 per opening
Adding or removing a fireplace	Starting at $90
Modifying a non-bearing wall or room	$65 per room
Changing exterior walls from 2"x4" to 2"x6"	Starting at $200
Redesigning a bathroom or a kitchen	Starting at $120
Reverse plan right reading	Quote required
Adapting plans for local building code requirements	Quote required
Engineering and Architectural stamping and services	Quote required
Adjust plan for handicapped accessibility	Quote required
Interactive Illustrations (choices of exterior materials)	Quote required
Metric conversion of home plan	Starting at $400

*Prices and Terms are subject to change without notice.

Paint-By-Number Wall Murals

Jungle #75014

Flamingo Island #76703

Treehouse #76304

Fish Friends #76704

Photo colors may vary from kit colors

Create a unique room with **WALL ART**™

You will be the envy of friends when you decorate with a Paint-By-Number Wall Mural.

Choose from over 100 custom designs for all ages and transform your room into a paradise.

You don't have to be an artist to paint a Wall Art mural. The whole family can participate in this fun and easy weekend project.

Your Wall Art kit includes everything but the wall!

Wall Art murals are available in a variety of sizes starting at the *low price of $49.97*.

ORDER TODAY!

It's As Easy As 1 - 2 - 3!

1. Tape   2. Trace   3. Paint

To order or request a catalog, call toll free

1-877-WALLMURAL (925-5687)

24 hours a day, 7 days a week, or buy online at

www.wallartdesigns.com

4

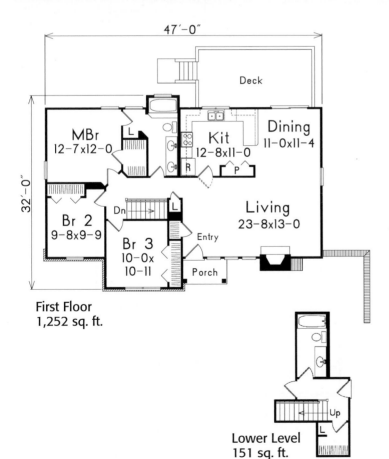

47'-0"

32'-0"

Deck

MBr
12-7x12-0

L

Kit
12-8x11-0

Dining
11-0x11-4

R

P

Br 2
9-8x9-9

Dn

L

Living
23-8x13-0

Br 3
10-0x
10-11

Entry

Porch

First Floor
1,252 sq. ft.

Up

L

Lower Level
151 sq. ft.

Plan #532-007D-0037
Price Code A
Total Living Area: 1,403 Sq. Ft.

Home has 3 bedrooms, 2 baths, 2-car drive under garage, second bath on lower level and basement foundation.

Special features
- Impressive living areas for a modest-sized home
- Special master/hall bath has linen storage, step-up tub and lots of window light
- Spacious closets everywhere you look

LOWE'S

Signature SERIES

Second Floor
632 sq. ft.

First Floor
1,441 sq. ft.

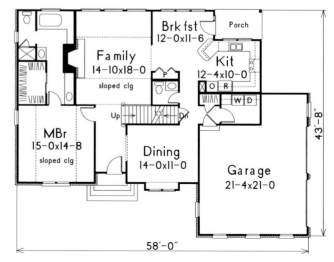

Plan #532-040D-0007
Price Code D

Total Living Area: 2,073 Sq. Ft.

Home has 4 bedrooms, 2 1/2 baths, 2-car side entry garage and basement foundation.

Special features
- Family room provides an ideal gathering area with a fireplace, large windows and vaulted ceiling
- Private first floor master bedroom suite with a vaulted ceiling and luxury bath
- Kitchen features angled bar connecting kitchen and breakfast area

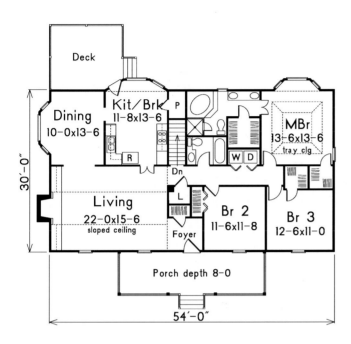

Deck

Dining 10-0x13-6

Kit/Brk 11-8x13-6

P

MBr 13-6x13-6 tray clg

W D

Dn

Living 22-0x15-6 sloped ceiling

L

Br 2 11-6x11-8

Br 3 12-6x11-0

Foyer

Porch depth 8-0

30'-0"

54'-0"

R

Plan #532-053D-0002
Price Code C

Total Living Area: 1,668 Sq. Ft.

Home has 3 bedrooms, 2 baths, 2-car drive under garage and basement foundation.

Special features
- Large bay windows grace the breakfast area, master bedroom and dining room
- Extensive walk-in closets and storage spaces throughout the home
- Handy covered entry porch
- Large living room has fireplace, built-in bookshelves and sloped ceiling

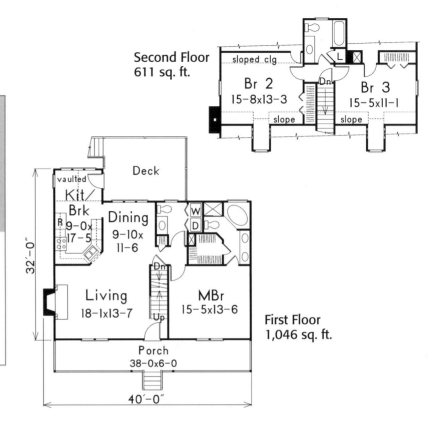

Second Floor
611 sq. ft.

sloped clg

Br 2
15-8x13-3

Br 3
15-5x11-1

slope

slope

Deck

vaulted

Kit/
Brk
9-0x
17-5

Dining
9-10x
11-6

W D

Living
18-1x13-7

MBr
15-5x13-6

First Floor
1,046 sq. ft.

Porch
38-0x6-0

32'-0"

40'-0"

Plan #532-053D-0030
Price Code B

Total Living Area: 1,657 Sq. Ft.

Home has 3 bedrooms, 2 1/2 baths, 2-car drive under garage and basement foundation.

Special features

■ Stylish pass-through between living and dining areas

■ Master bedroom is secluded from living area for privacy

■ Large windows in breakfast and dining areas

Plan #532-003D-0005
Price Code B

Total Living Area: 1,708 Sq. Ft.

Home has 3 bedrooms, 2 baths, 2-car garage and basement foundation, drawings also include crawl space foundation.

Special features

- Massive family room is enhanced with several windows, a fireplace and access to the porch
- Deluxe master bath is accented by a step-up corner tub flanked by double vanities
- Closets throughout maintain organized living
- Bedrooms are isolated from living areas

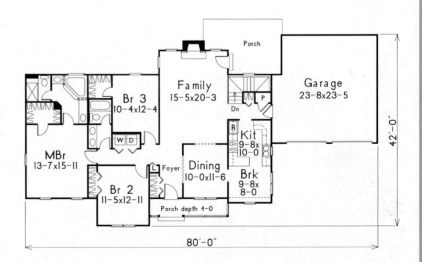

Plan #532-007D-0017
Price Code C

Total Living Area: 1,882 Sq. Ft.

Home has 4 bedrooms, 2 baths, 2-car side entry garage and basement foundation.

Special features

■ Handsome brick facade

■ Spacious great room and dining area combination is brightened by unique corner windows and patio access

■ Well-designed kitchen incorporates a breakfast bar peninsula, sweeping casement window above sink and walk-in pantry island

■ Master bedroom features a large walk-in closet and private bath with bay window

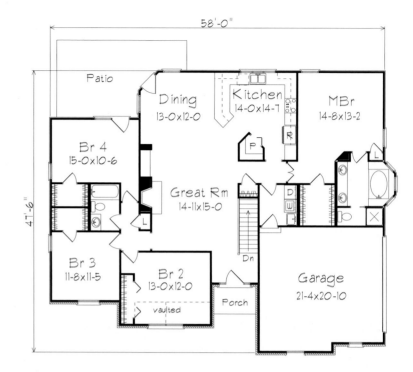

Comfortable Family Living In This Ranch

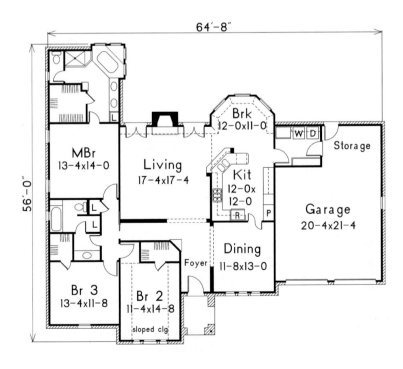

Plan #532-037D-0020
Price Code D
Total Living Area: 1,994 Sq. Ft.

Home has 3 bedrooms, 2 baths, 2-car garage and slab foundation.

Special features
- Convenient entrance from the garage into the main living area through the utility room
- Standard 9' ceilings, bedroom #2 features a 12' vaulted ceiling and a 10' ceiling in the dining room
- Master bedroom offers a full bath with oversized tub, separate shower and walk-in closet
- Entry leads to formal dining room and attractive living room with double French doors and fireplace

LOWE'S

Signature SERIES

66'-0"

54'-0"

Porch depth 6-0

MBr
13-4x14-4

Brm

Stor.

Stor.

D W P

Up

Garage
21-8x25-2

Brk
10-0x8-0

Kit
13-2x11-0

Dining
13-2x11-4

Porch

skylt

Living
16-0x17-0

Br 3
10-8x11-8

Br 2
10-8x
13-2

Plan #532-021D-0011
Price Code D
Total Living Area: 1,800 Sq. Ft.

Home has 3 bedrooms, 2 baths, 2-car side entry garage and crawl space foundation, drawings also include slab foundation.

Special features

- Energy efficient home with 2" x 6" exterior walls

- Covered front and rear porches add outdoor living area

- 12' ceilings in the kitchen, breakfast area, dining and living rooms

- Private master bedroom features an expansive bath

- Side entry garage has two storage areas

- Pillared styling with brick and stucco exterior finish

Plan #532-007D-0055
Price Code D
Total Living Area: 2,029 Sq. Ft.

Home has 3 bedrooms, 2 baths, 2-car side entry garage and basement foundation, drawings also include crawl space and slab foundations.

Special features

■ Stonework, gables, roof dormer and double porches create a country flavor

■ Kitchen enjoys extravagant cabinetry and counterspace in a bay, island snack bar, built-in pantry and cheery dining area with multiple tall windows

■ Angled stair descends from large entry with wood columns and is open to vaulted great room with corner fireplace

■ Master bedroom boasts two walk-in closets, a private bath with double-door entry and a secluded porch

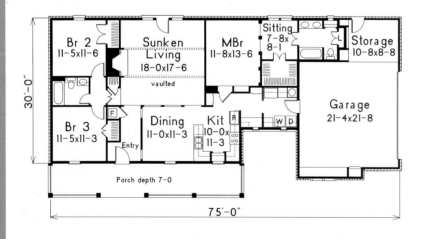

Plan #532-021D-0006
Price Code C

Total Living Area: 1,600 Sq. Ft.

Home has 3 bedrooms, 2 baths, 2-car side entry garage and slab foundation, drawings also include crawl space and basement foundations.

Special features

- Energy efficient home with 2" x 6" exterior walls

- Impressive sunken living room features a massive stone fireplace and 16' vaulted ceiling

- The dining room is conveniently located next to the kitchen and divided for privacy

- Special amenities include a sewing room, glass shelves in kitchen and master bath and a large utility area

- Sunken master bedroom features a distinctive sitting room

Rambling Country Bungalow

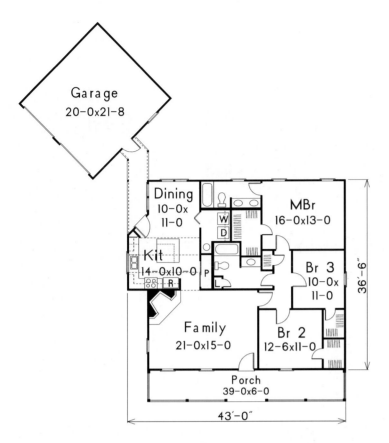

Plan #532-040D-0003
Price Code B

Total Living Area: 1,475 Sq. Ft.

Home has 3 bedrooms, 2 baths, 2-car detached side entry garage and slab foundation, drawings also include crawl space foundation.

Special features

- Family room features a high ceiling and prominent corner fireplace
- Kitchen with island counter and garden window makes a convenient connection between the family and dining rooms
- Hallway leads to three bedrooms all with large walk-in closets
- Covered breezeway joins main house and garage
- Full-width covered porch entry lends a country touch

LOWE'S

Signature SERIES

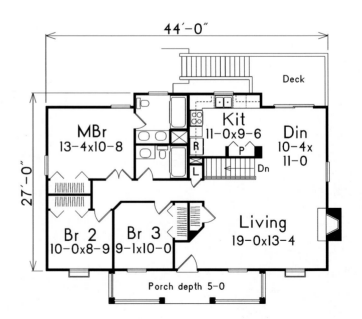

Plan #532-007D-0030
Price Code AA

Total Living Area: 1,140 Sq. Ft.

Home has 3 bedrooms, 2 baths, 2-car drive under garage and basement foundation.

Special features

- Open and spacious living and dining areas for family gatherings
- Well-organized kitchen with an abundance of cabinetry and a built-in pantry
- Roomy master bath features a double-bowl vanity

44'-0"

27'-0"

Deck

MBr
13-4x10-8

Kit
11-0x9-6

Din
10-4x
11-0

R

P

L

Dn

Br 2
10-0x8-9

Br 3
9-1x10-0

Living
19-0x13-4

Porch depth 5-0

Convenient Ranch

Plan #532-001D-0093
Price Code AA

Total Living Area: 1,120 Sq. Ft.

Home has 3 bedrooms, 1 1/2 baths and crawl space foundation, drawings also include basement and slab foundations.

Special features
- Master bedroom includes a half bath with laundry area, linen closet and kitchen access
- Kitchen has charming double-door entry, breakfast bar and a convenient walk-in pantry
- Welcoming front porch opens to large living room with coat closet

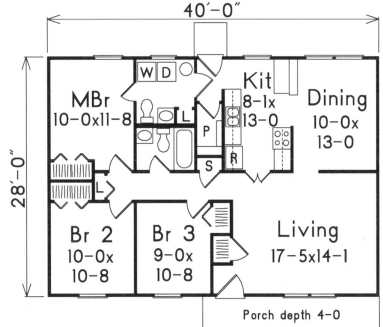

40'-0"

28'-0"

MBr
10-0x11-8

W D

Kit
8-1x
13-0

Dining
10-0x
13-0

L

P

S R

Br 2
10-0x
10-8

Br 3
9-0x
10-8

Living
17-5x14-1

Porch depth 4-0

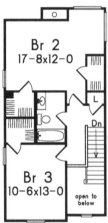

Br 2
17–8x12–0

Br 3
10–6x13–0

open to below

L

Dn

Second Floor
573 sq. ft.

Plan #532-007D-0038
Price Code B

Total Living Area: 1,524 Sq. Ft.

Home has 3 bedrooms, 2 1/2 baths, 2-car garage and basement foundation, drawings also include crawl space and slab foundations.

Special features

■ Delightful balcony overlooks two-story entry illuminated by oval window

■ Roomy first floor master bedroom offers quiet privacy

■ All bedrooms feature one or more walk-in closets

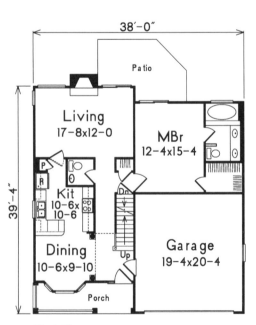

38'–0"

Patio

Living
17–8x12–0

MBr
12–4x15–4

39'–4"

Kit
10–6x
10–6

P

R

Dn

Up

Dining
10–6x9–10

Garage
19–4x20–4

Porch

First Floor
951 sq. ft.

Plan #532-001D-0048
Price Code A

Total Living Area: 1,400 Sq. Ft.

Home has 3 bedrooms, 2 baths, 2-car garage and crawl space foundation, drawings also include basement and slab foundations.

Special features

- Front porch offers warmth and welcome
- Large great room opens into dining room creating an open living atmosphere
- Kitchen features convenient laundry area, pantry and breakfast bar

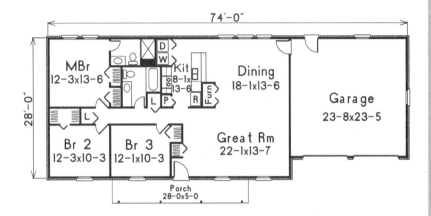

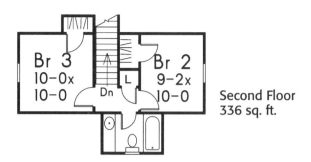

Br 3
10-0x
10-0

L

Br 2
9-2x
10-0

Dn

Second Floor
336 sq. ft.

Plan #532-045D-0017
Price Code AA

Total Living Area: 954 Sq. Ft.

Home has 3 bedrooms, 2 baths and basement foundation.

Special features

- Kitchen has cozy bayed eating area
- Master bedroom has a walk-in closet and private bath
- Large great room has access to the back porch
- Convenient coat closet near front entry

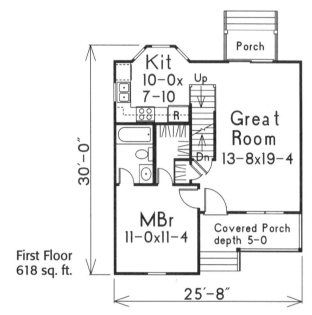

Porch

Kit
10-0x
7-10

Up

R

Great
Room
13-8x19-4

Dn

30'-0"

MBr
11-0x11-4

Covered Porch
depth 5-0

First Floor
618 sq. ft.

25'-8"

Plan #532-053D-0041
Price Code A
Total Living Area: 1,364 Sq. Ft.

Home has 3 bedrooms, 2 baths, 2-car drive under garage and basement foundation.

Special features
- Master bedroom includes a full bath
- Pass-through kitchen opens into breakfast room with laundry closet and access to deck
- Adjoining dining and living rooms with vaulted ceilings and a fireplace create an open living area
- Dining room features large bay window

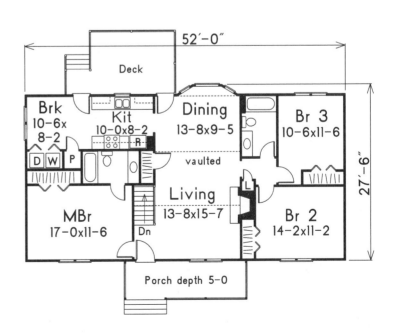

SPARR

Plan #532-001D-0086
Price Code AA

Total Living Area: 1,154 Sq. Ft.

Home has 3 bedrooms, 1 1/2 baths and crawl space foundation, drawings also include slab foundation.

Special features

- U-shaped kitchen features a large breakfast bar and handy laundry area

- Private second floor bedrooms share half bath

- Large living/dining area opens to deck

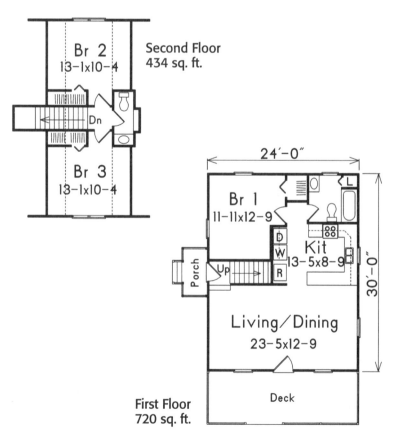

Br 2
13-1x10-4

Second Floor
434 sq. ft.

Dn

Br 3
13-1x10-4

24'-0"

Br 1
11-11x12-9

Kit
13-5x8-9

Porch

Up

30'-0"

Living/Dining
23-5x12-9

First Floor
720 sq. ft.

Deck

Plan #532-007D-0010
Price Code C

Total Living Area: 1,721 Sq. Ft.

Home has 3 bedrooms, 2 baths, 3-car garage and walk-out basement foundation, drawings also include crawl space and slab foundations.

Special features

- Roof dormers add great curb appeal
- Vaulted dining and great rooms are immersed in light from the atrium window wall
- Breakfast room opens onto the covered porch
- Functionally designed kitchen

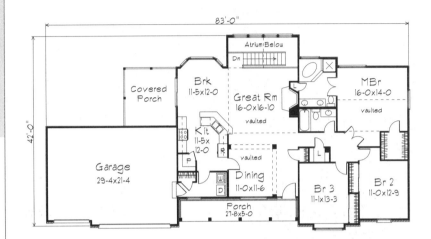

Rear View

Plan #532-007D-0103
Price Code A

Total Living Area: 1,231 Sq. Ft.

Home has 2 bedrooms, 2 baths, 1-car drive under garage and walk-out basement foundation.

Special features

- Dutch gables and stone accents provide an enchanting appearance
- The spacious living room offers a masonry fireplace, atrium with window wall and is open to a dining area with bay window
- Kitchen has a breakfast counter, lots of cabinet space and glass sliding doors to a balcony
- 380 square feet of optional living area on the lower level

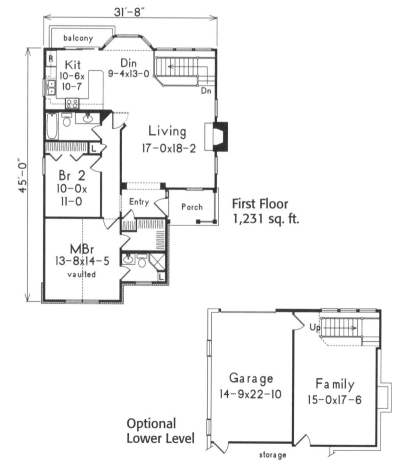

31'-8"

balcony

Kit
10-6x
10-7

Din
9-4x13-0

Dn

Living
17-0x18-2

45'-0"

Br 2
10-0x
11-0

Entry

Porch

MBr
13-8x14-5
vaulted

First Floor
1,231 sq. ft.

Up

Garage
14-9x22-10

Family
15-0x17-6

Optional
Lower Level

storage

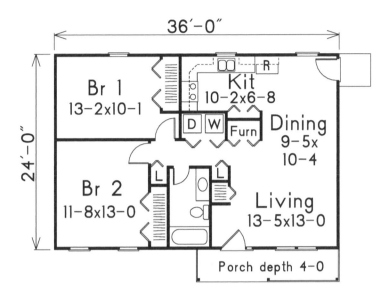

Plan #532-001D-0040
Price Code AAA

Total Living Area: 864 Sq. Ft.

Home has 2 bedrooms, 1 bath and crawl space foundation, drawings also include basement and slab foundations.

Special features

- L-shaped kitchen with convenient pantry is adjacent to dining area
- Easy access to laundry area, linen closet and storage closet
- Both bedrooms include ample closet space

Plan #532-022D-0002
Price Code A

Total Living Area: 1,246 Sq. Ft.

Home has 3 bedrooms, 2 baths, 2-car garage and basement foundation.

Special features

- Corner living room window adds openness and light
- Out-of-the-way kitchen with dining area accesses the outdoors
- Private first floor master bedroom has a corner window
- Large walk-in closet is located in bedroom #3
- Easily built perimeter allows economical construction

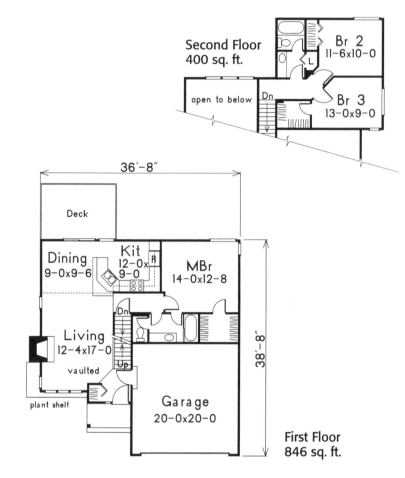

Second Floor
400 sq. ft.

Br 2
11-6x10-0

open to below   Dn

Br 3
13-0x9-0

36´-8˝

Deck

Dining
9-0x9-6

Kit
12-0x
9-0

MBr
14-0x12-8

Dn

Living
12-4x17-0

vaulted

Up

plant shelf

Garage
20-0x20-0

38´-8˝

First Floor
846 sq. ft.

Plan #532-018D-0008
Price Code C
Total Living Area: 2,109 Sq. Ft.

Home has 3 bedrooms, 2 baths, 2-car side entry garage and slab foundation, drawings also include crawl space foundation.

Special features
- 12' ceilings in living and dining rooms
- Kitchen designed as an integral part of the family and breakfast rooms
- The secluded and generously sized master bedroom includes a plant shelf, walk-in closet and private bath with separate tub and shower
- Stately columns and circle-top window frame dining room

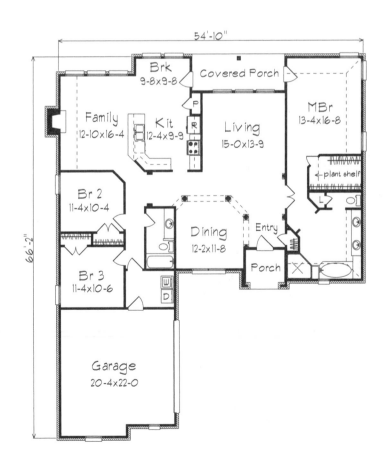

LOWE'S

Signature SERIES

Plan #532-001D-0064
Price Code D

Total Living Area: 2,262 Sq. Ft.

Home has 3 bedrooms, 2 1/2 baths, 2-car rear entry garage and crawl space foundation, drawings also include basement and slab foundations.

Special features

■ Charming exterior features include large front porch, two patios, front balcony and double bay windows

■ Den provides an impressive entry to a sunken family room

■ Conveniently located first floor laundry

■ Large master bedroom has a walk-in closet, dressing area and bath

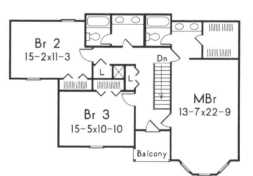

Second Floor
1,135 sq. ft.

Br 2
15-2x11-3

Br 3
15-5x10-10

Dn

MBr
13-7x22-9

Balcony

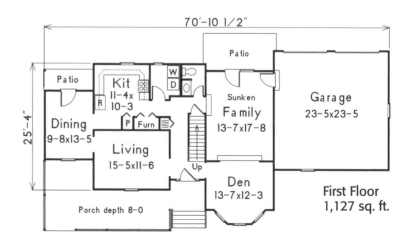

70'-10 1/2"

25'-4"

Patio

Patio

Kit
11-4x
10-3

R

W
D

Sunken
Family
13-7x17-8

Garage
23-5x23-5

Dining
9-8x13-5

P   Furn

Living
15-5x11-6

Up

Den
13-7x12-3

Porch depth 8-0

First Floor
1,127 sq. ft.

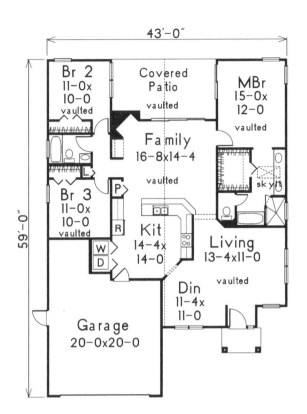

43'-0"

Br 2
11-0x
10-0
vaulted

Covered Patio
vaulted

MBr
15-0x
12-0
vaulted

Family
16-8x14-4
vaulted

P
R

Br 3
11-0x
10-0
vaulted

Kit
14-4x
14-0

Living
13-4x11-0
vaulted

sky lt

W
D

Din
11-4x
11-0

59'-0"

Garage
20-0x20-0

Plan #532-048D-0011
Price Code B
Total Living Area: 1,550 Sq. Ft.

Home has 3 bedrooms, 2 baths, 2-car garage and slab foundation.

Special features

- Cozy corner fireplace provides focal point in family room
- Master bedroom features large walk-in closet, skylight and separate tub and shower
- Convenient laundry closet
- Kitchen with pantry and breakfast bar connects to family room
- Family room and master bedroom access covered patio

Signature SERIES

Plan #532-040D-0001
Price Code D

Total Living Area: 1,814 Sq. Ft.

Home has 3 bedrooms, 2 1/2 baths, 2-car detached side entry garage and crawl space foundation, drawings also include slab foundation.

Special features

■ Large master bedroom includes a spacious bath with garden tub, separate shower and large walk-in closet

■ The spacious kitchen and dining area are brightened by large windows and patio access

■ Detached two-car garage with walkway leading to house adds charm to this country home

■ Large front porch

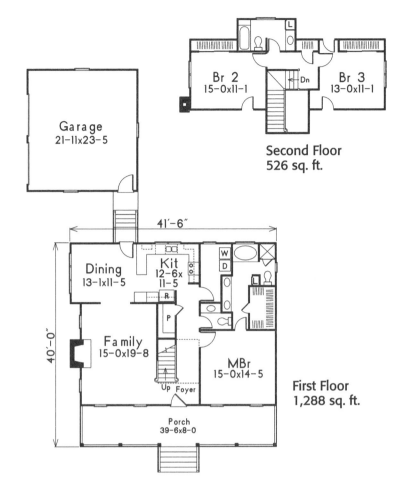

Garage
21-11x23-5

Br 2
15-0x11-1

Dn

Br 3
13-0x11-1

Second Floor
526 sq. ft.

41'-6"

40'-0"

Dining
13-1x11-5

Kit
12-6x
11-5

W
D

R
P

Family
15-0x19-8

MBr
15-0x14-5

Up Foyer

First Floor
1,288 sq. ft.

Porch
39-6x8-0

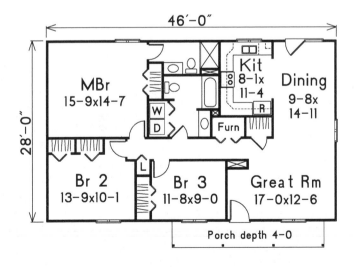

46'-0"

28'-0"

MBr
15-9x14-7

Kit
8-1x
11-4

Dining
9-8x
14-11

W
D

R

Furn

Br 2
13-9x10-1

L

Br 3
11-8x9-0

Great Rm
17-0x12-6

Porch depth 4-0

Plan #532-001D-0072
Price Code A

Total Living Area: 1,288 Sq. Ft.

Home has 3 bedrooms, 2 baths and crawl space foundation, drawings also include basement and slab foundations.

Special features

■ Kitchen, dining area and great room join to create an open living space

■ Master bedroom includes private bath

■ Secondary bedrooms include ample closet space

■ Hall bath features convenient laundry closet

■ Dining room accesses the outdoors

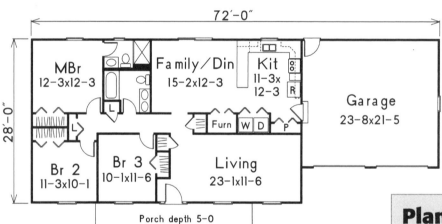

72'-0"

28'-0"

MBr
12-3x12-3

Family/Din
15-2x12-3

Kit
11-3x
12-3

Garage
23-8x21-5

Br 2
11-3x10-1

Br 3
10-1x11-6

Living
23-1x11-6

Furn W D P

Porch depth 5-0

Plan #532-001D-0053
Price Code A
Total Living Area: 1,344 Sq. Ft.

Home has 3 bedrooms, 2 baths, 2-car garage and crawl space foundation, drawings also include basement and slab foundations.

Special features

■ Family/dining room has sliding glass doors to the outdoors

■ Master bedroom features a private bath

■ Hall bath includes double vanity for added convenience

■ U-shaped kitchen features a large pantry and laundry area

LOWE'S

Signature SERIES

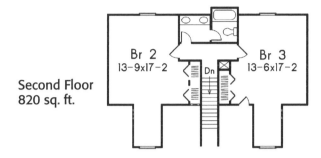

Second Floor
820 sq. ft.

Br 2
13-9x17-2

Dn

Br 3
13-6x17-2

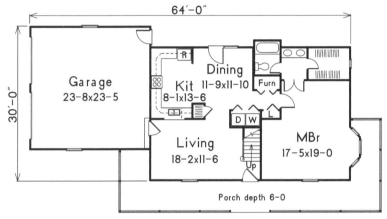

64'-0"

30'-0"

Garage
23-8x23-5

R

Dining
11-9x11-10

Kit
8-1x13-6

Furn

D W

L

Living
18-2x11-6

Up

MBr
17-5x19-0

Porch depth 6-0

First Floor
1,055 sq. ft.

Plan #532-001D-0061
Price Code C
Total Living Area: 1,875 Sq. Ft.

Home has 3 bedrooms, 2 baths, 2-car side entry garage and crawl space foundation, drawings also include basement and slab foundations.

Special features
- Country-style exterior with wrap-around porch and dormers
- Large second floor bedrooms share a dressing area and bath
- Master bedroom includes a bay window, walk-in closet, dressing area and bath

LOWE'S

Signature
SERIES

Plan #532-001D-0050
Price Code C

Total Living Area: 1,827 Sq. Ft.

Home has 4 bedrooms, 2 baths, 2-car garage and crawl space foundation, drawings also include basement and slab foundations.

Special features

■ Two large bedrooms are located on the second floor for extra privacy, plus two bedrooms on the first floor

■ L-shaped kitchen is adjacent to the family room

■ Ample closet space in all bedrooms

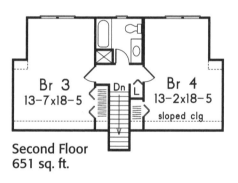

Br 3
13-7x18-5

Dn L

Br 4
13-2x18-5

sloped clg

Second Floor
651 sq. ft.

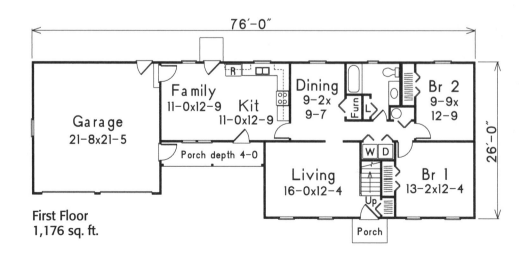

76'-0"

Family
11-0x12-9

Kit
11-0x12-9

Dining
9-2x
9-7

Br 2
9-9x
12-9

Furn L

Garage
21-8x21-5

Porch depth 4-0

W D

Living
16-0x12-4

Br 1
13-2x12-4

Up

26'-0"

Porch

First Floor
1,176 sq. ft.

Plan #532-003D-0002
Price Code B

Total Living Area: 1,676 Sq. Ft.

Home has 3 bedrooms, 2 baths, 2-car garage and basement foundation, drawings also include crawl space and slab foundations.

Special features

- The living area skylights and large breakfast room with bay window provide plenty of sunlight

- The master bedroom has a walk-in closet and both the secondary bedrooms have large closets

- Vaulted ceilings, plant shelving and a fireplace provide a quality living area

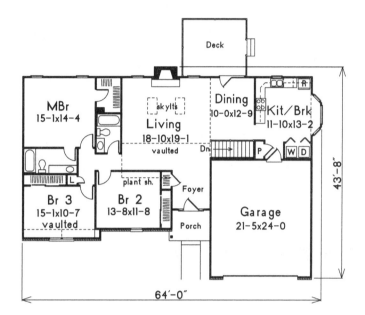

LOWE'S *Signature* SERIES

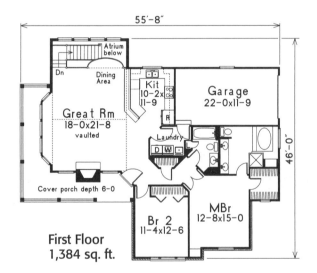

Rear View

Plan #532-007D-0068
Price Code B
Total Living Area: 1,384 Sq. Ft.

Home has 2 bedrooms, 2 baths, 1-car side entry garage and walk-out basement foundation.

Special features

- Wrap-around country porch for peaceful evenings
- Vaulted great room enjoys a large bay window, stone fireplace, pass-through kitchen and awesome rear views through atrium window wall
- Master bedroom features a double-door entry, walk-in closet and a fabulous bath
- Atrium opens to 611 square feet of optional living area below

55'-8"

Atrium below

Dn

Dining Area

Kit 10-2x 11-9

Garage 22-0x11-9

Great Rm 18-0x21-8 vaulted

Laundry

D W

46'-0"

Cover porch depth 6-0

Br 2 11-4x12-6

MBr 12-8x15-0

First Floor 1,384 sq. ft.

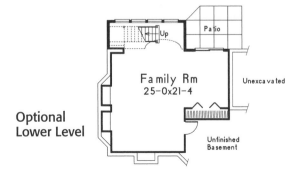

Up

Patio

Family Rm 25-0x21-4

Unexcavated

Optional Lower Level

Unfinished Basement

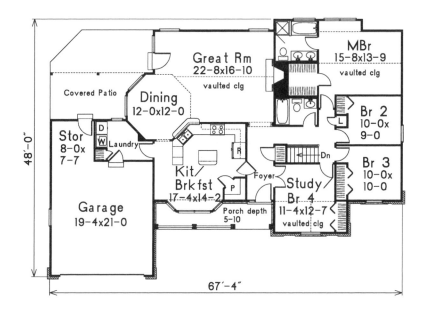

Great Rm
22-8x16-10
vaulted clg

MBr
15-8x13-9
vaulted clg

Covered Patio

Dining
12-0x12-0

Stor
8-0x
7-7

D
W
Laundry

Br 2
10-0x
9-0

Garage
19-4x21-0

Kit/
Brkfst
17-4x14-2

R

P

Foyer

Dn

Br 3
10-0x
10-0

Study
Br 4
11-4x12-7
vaulted clg

Porch depth
5-10

48'-0"

67'-4"

Plan #532-007D-0049
Price Code C

Total Living Area: 1,791 Sq. Ft.

Home has 4 bedrooms, 2 baths, 2-car garage with storage and basement foundation, drawings also include crawl space and slab foundations.

Special features

- Vaulted great room and octagon-shaped dining area enjoy views of covered patio

- Kitchen features a pass-through to dining area, center island, large walk-in pantry and breakfast room with large bay window

- Master bedroom is vaulted with sitting area

Signature SERIES

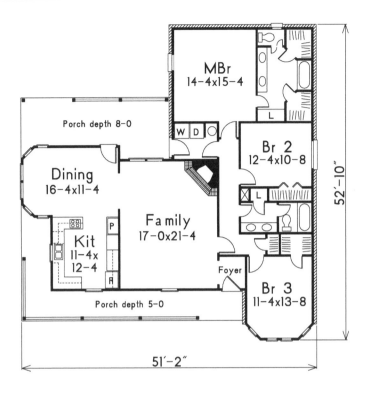

Porch depth 8-0

MBr
14-4x15-4

W D

Dining
16-4x11-4

Kit
11-4x
12-4

P

R

Family
17-0x21-4

Foyer

Br 2
12-4x10-8

L

L

Br 3
11-4x13-8

Porch depth 5-0

52'-10"

51'-2"

Plan #532-037D-0006
Price Code C

Total Living Area: 1,772 Sq. Ft.

Home has 3 bedrooms, 2 baths, 2-car detached garage and slab foundation, drawings also include crawl space foundation.

Special features

- Extended porches in front and rear provide a charming touch
- Large bay windows lend distinction to dining room and bedroom #3
- Efficient U-shaped kitchen
- Master bedroom includes two walk-in closets
- Full corner fireplace in family room

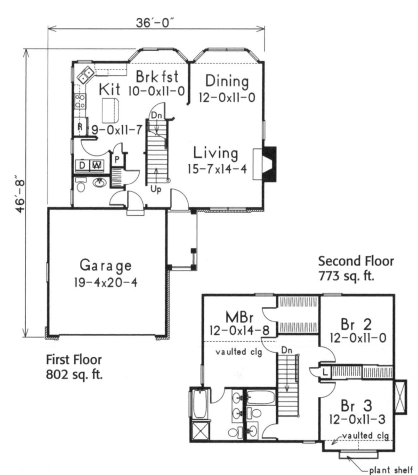

First Floor
802 sq. ft.

Second Floor
773 sq. ft.

Plan #532-007D-0054
Price Code B

Total Living Area: 1,575 Sq. Ft.

Home has 3 bedrooms, 2 1/2 baths, 2-car garage and basement foundation, drawings also include crawl space and slab foundations.

Special features
- ■ Inviting porch leads to spacious living and dining rooms
- ■ Kitchen with corner windows features an island snack bar, attractive breakfast room bay, convenient laundry and built-in pantry
- ■ A luxury bath and walk-in closet adorn master bedroom suite

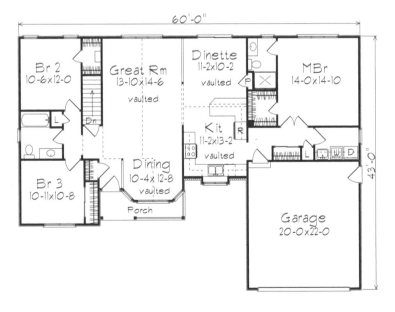

Plan #532-033D-0012
Price Code C

Total Living Area: 1,546 Sq. Ft.

Home has 3 bedrooms, 2 baths, 2-car garage and basement foundation.

Special features

- Spacious, open rooms create a casual atmosphere
- Master bedroom is secluded for privacy
- Dining room features large bay window
- Kitchen and dinette combine for added space and include access to the outdoors
- Large laundry room includes a convenient sink

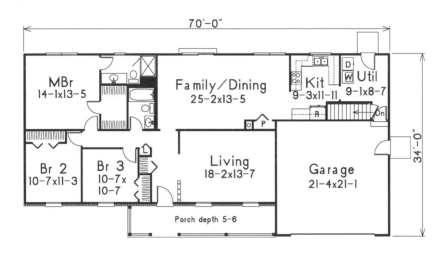

70'-0"

MBr
14-1x13-5

Family/Dining
25-2x13-5

Kit
9-3x11-11

Util
9-1x8-7

34'-0"

Br 2
10-7x11-3

Br 3
10-7x
10-7

Living
18-2x13-7

Garage
21-4x21-1

Porch depth 5-6

Plan #532-008D-0004
Price Code B

Total Living Area: 1,643 Sq. Ft.

Home has 3 bedrooms, 2 baths, 2-car garage and basement foundation, drawings also include crawl space and slab foundations.

Special features

■ An attractive front entry porch gives this ranch a country accent

■ Spacious family/dining room is the focal point of this design

■ Kitchen and utility room are conveniently located near gathering areas

■ Formal living room in the front of the home provides area for quiet and privacy

■ Master bedroom has view to the rear of the home and a generous walk-in closet

LOWE'S

Signature
SERIES

Plan #532-037D-0016
Price Code C

Total Living Area: 2,066 Sq. Ft.

Home has 3 bedrooms, 2 1/2 baths, optional 2-car side entry garage and slab foundation.

Special features

- Large master bedroom includes sitting area and private bath
- Open living room features a fireplace with built-in bookshelves
- Spacious kitchen accesses formal dining area and breakfast room

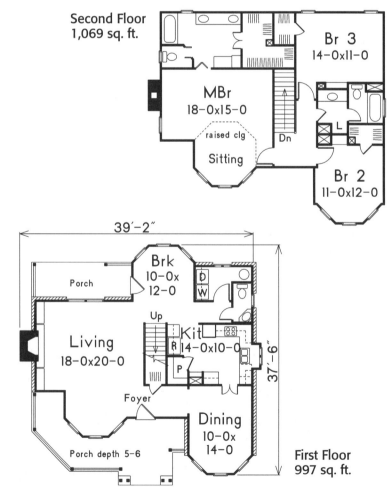

Second Floor
1,069 sq. ft.

Br 3
14-0x11-0

MBr
18-0x15-0

raised clg

Dn

Sitting

Br 2
11-0x12-0

39'-2"

Porch

Brk
10-0x
12-0

D
W

Up

Living
18-0x20-0

Kit
14-0x10-0

R

P

Foyer

Dining
10-0x
14-0

Porch depth 5-6

37'-6"

First Floor
997 sq. ft.

Plan #532-058D-0033
Price Code A

Total Living Area: 1,440 Sq. Ft.

Home has 2 bedrooms, 2 baths, 2-car side entry garage and basement foundation.

Special features

- Open floor plan with access to covered porches in front and back
- Lots of linen, pantry and closet space throughout
- Laundry/mud room between kitchen and garage is a convenient feature

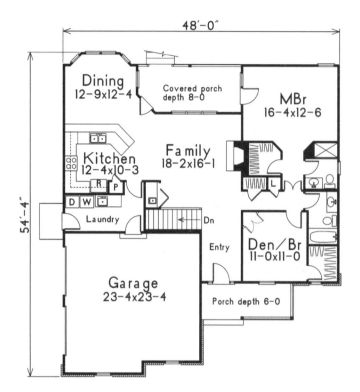

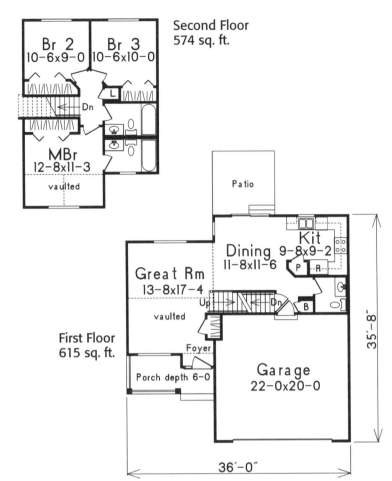

Second Floor
574 sq. ft.

Br 2
10-6x9-0

Br 3
10-6x10-0

Dn
L

MBr
12-8x11-3

vaulted

Plan #532-041D-0006
Price Code AA

Total Living Area: 1,189 Sq. Ft.

Home has 3 bedrooms, 2 1/2 baths, 2-car garage and basement foundation.

Special features

■ All bedrooms are located on the second floor

■ Dining room and kitchen both have views of the patio

■ Convenient half bath located near the kitchen

■ Master bedroom has a private bath

Patio

Kit
9-8x9-2

Dining
11-8x11-6

P   R

Great Rm
13-8x17-4

Up   Dn   B

vaulted

First Floor
615 sq. ft.

Foyer

Porch depth 6-0

Garage
22-0x20-0

35'-8"

36'-0"

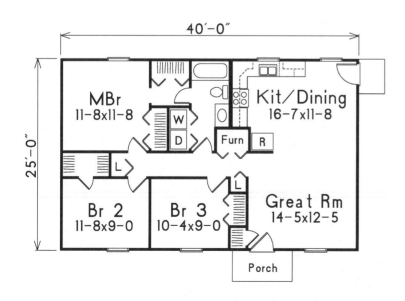

Plan #532-001D-0041
Price Code AA

Total Living Area: 1,000 Sq. Ft.

Home has 3 bedrooms, 1 bath and crawl space foundation, drawings also include basement and slab foundations.

Special features

- Bath includes convenient closeted laundry area
- Master bedroom includes double closets and private access to bath
- The foyer features a handy coat closet
- L-shaped kitchen provides easy access outdoors

Plan #532-001D-0024
Price Code A

Total Living Area: 1,360 Sq. Ft.

Home has 3 bedrooms, 2 baths, 2-car side entry garage and basement foundation, drawings also include crawl space and slab foundations.

Special features

- Kitchen/dining room features island workspace and plenty of dining area
- Master bedroom has a large walk-in closet and private bath
- Laundry room is adjacent to the kitchen for easy access
- Convenient workshop in garage
- Large closets in secondary bedrooms

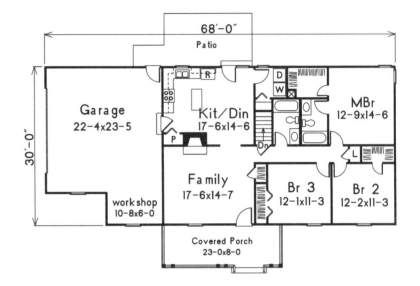

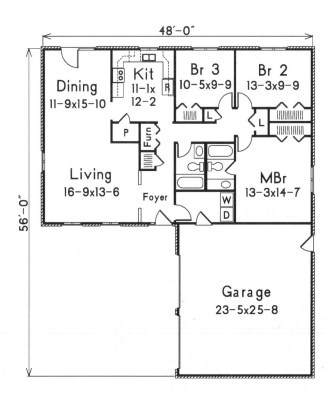

Plan #532-001D-0071
Price Code A

Total Living Area: 1,440 Sq. Ft.

Home has 3 bedrooms, 2 baths, 2-car side entry garage and crawl space foundation, drawings also include basement and slab foundations.

Special features

- Spaciousness is created with open living and dining areas
- Entry foyer features a coat closet and half wall leading into the living area
- Walk-in pantry adds convenience to the U-shaped kitchen
- Spacious utility room is adjacent to the garage

Floor plan dimensions and rooms:

48'-0" (width), 56'-0" (depth)

- Dining 11-9x15-10
- Kit 11-1x 12-2
- Br 3 10-5x9-9
- Br 2 13-3x9-9
- Living 16-9x13-6
- Foyer
- MBr 13-3x14-7
- Garage 23-5x25-8

Signature SERIES

Plan #532-007D-0102
Price Code A

Total Living Area: 1,452 Sq. Ft.

Home has 4 bedrooms, 2 baths and basement foundation.

Special features

- Large living room features a cozy corner fireplace, bayed dining area and access from entry with guest closet

- Forward master bedroom enjoys having its own bath and linen closet

- Three additional bedrooms share a bath with double-bowl vanity

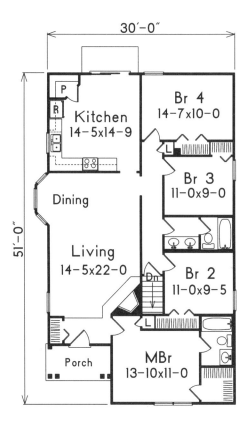

30'-0"

51'-0"

Kitchen
14-5x14-9

Br 4
14-7x10-0

Dining

Br 3
11-0x9-0

Living
14-5x22-0

Br 2
11-0x9-5

Porch

MBr
13-10x11-0

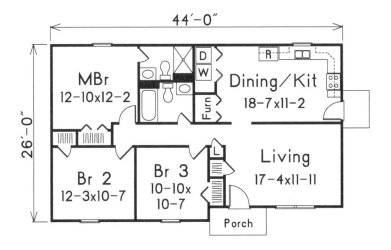

44'-0"

26'-0"

MBr
12-10x12-2

Dining/Kit
18-7x11-2

D
W

Furn

R

Br 2
12-3x10-7

Br 3
10-10x
10-7

L

Living
17-4x11-11

Porch

Plan #532-001D-0043
Price Code AA

Total Living Area: 1,104 Sq. Ft.

Home has 3 bedrooms, 2 baths and crawl space foundation, drawings also include basement and slab foundations.

Special features
- Master bedroom includes a private bath
- Convenient side entrance to the dining area/kitchen
- Laundry area is located near the kitchen
- Large living area creates a comfortable atmosphere

Plan #532-005D-0001

Price Code B

Total Living Area: 1,400 Sq. Ft.

Home has 3 bedrooms, 2 baths, 2-car garage and basement foundation, drawings also include crawl space foundation.

Special features

- Master bedroom is secluded for privacy
- Large utility room has additional cabinet space
- Covered porch provides an outdoor seating area
- Roof dormers add great curb appeal
- Living room and master bedroom feature vaulted ceilings
- Oversized two-car garage has storage space

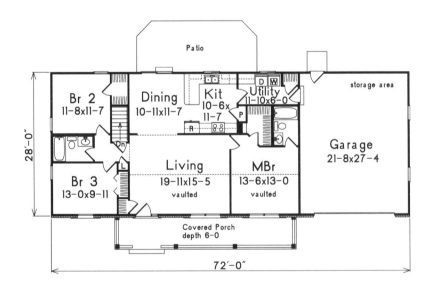

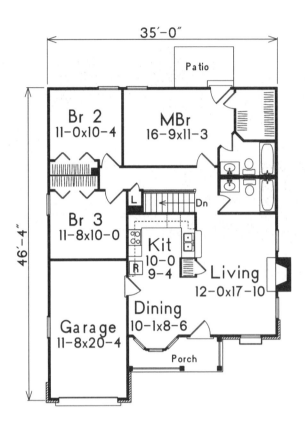

35'-0"

Patio

Br 2
11-0x10-4

MBr
16-9x11-3

46'-4"

Br 3
11-8x10-0

L

Dn

Kit
10-0
9-4

Living
12-0x17-10

Dining
10-1x8-6

Garage
11-8x20-4

Porch

Plan #532-007D-0110
Price Code AA
Total Living Area: 1,169 Sq. Ft.

Home has 3 bedrooms, 2 baths, 1-car garage and basement foundation.

Special features
- Front facade features a distinctive country appeal
- Living room enjoys a wood-burning fireplace and pass-through to kitchen
- A stylish U-shaped kitchen offers an abundance of cabinet and counter-space with view to living room
- A large walk-in closet, access to rear patio and private bath are many features of the master bedroom

Plan #532-007D-0050
Price Code E

Total Living Area: 2,723 Sq. Ft.

Home has 3 bedrooms, 2 1/2 baths, 3-car side entry garage and basement foundation.

Special features

- Large porch invites you into an elegant foyer which accesses a vaulted study with private hall and coat closet

- Great room is second to none, comprised of a fireplace, built-in shelves, vaulted ceiling and a 1 1/2 story window wall

- A spectacular hearth room with vaulted ceiling and masonry fireplace opens to an elaborate kitchen featuring two snack bars, a cooking island and walk-in pantry

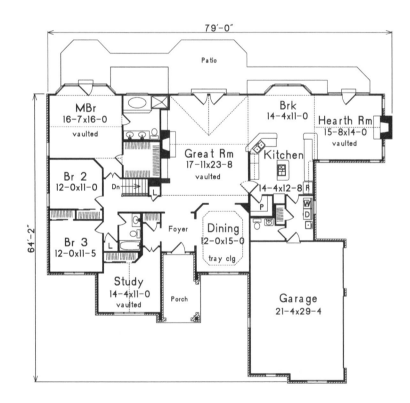

Plan #532-006D-0003
Price Code B

Total Living Area: 1,674 Sq. Ft.

Home has 3 bedrooms, 2 baths, 2-car garage and basement foundation, drawings also include crawl space and slab foundations.

Special features

- Vaulted great room, dining area and kitchen all enjoy a central fireplace and log bin
- Convenient laundry/mud room is located between the garage and family area with handy stairs to the basement
- Easily expandable screened porch and adjacent patio access the dining area
- Master bedroom features a full bath with tub, separate shower and walk-in closet

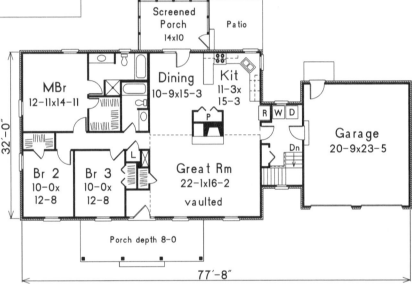

Distinctive Turret Surrounds The Dining Bay

Plan #532-018D-0006
Price Code B

Total Living Area: 1,742 Sq. Ft.

Home has 3 bedrooms, 2 baths, 2-car garage and slab foundation, drawings also include crawl space foundation.

Special features

■ Efficient kitchen combines with breakfast area and great room creating a spacious living area

■ Master bedroom includes a private bath with huge walk-in closet, shower and corner tub

■ Great room boasts a fireplace and access outdoors

■ Laundry room is conveniently located near the kitchen and garage

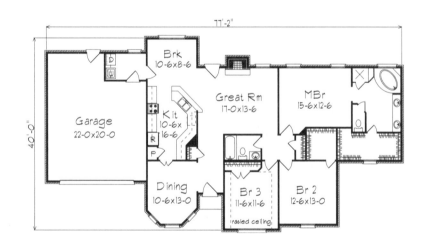

Plan #532-014D-0015
Price Code C

Total Living Area: 1,941 Sq. Ft.

Home has 3 bedrooms, 2 1/2 baths, 2-car garage and crawl space foundation.

Special features

■ Kitchen incorporates a cooktop island, a handy pantry and adjoins the dining and family rooms

■ Formal living room, to the left of the foyer, lends a touch of privacy

■ Raised ceilings in foyer, kitchen, dining and living areas

■ Laundry room, half bath and closet all located near the garage

■ Both the dining and family rooms have access outdoors through sliding doors

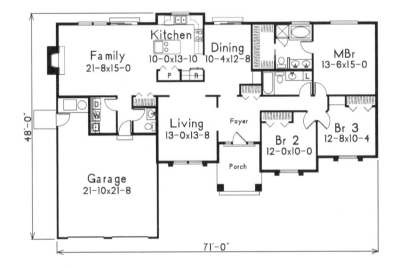

Plan #532-021D-0016
Price Code B

Total Living Area: 1,600 Sq. Ft.

Home has 3 bedrooms, 2 baths, 2-car side entry garage and crawl space foundation, drawings also include slab foundation.

Special features

- Energy efficient home with 2" x 6" exterior walls
- First floor master bedroom is accessible from two points of entry
- Master bath dressing area includes separate vanities and a mirrored makeup counter
- Second floor bedrooms have generous storage space and share a full bath

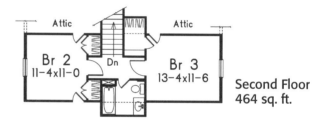

Second Floor
464 sq. ft.

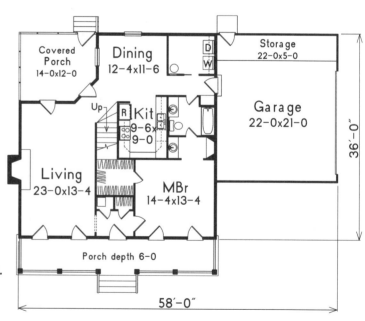

First Floor
1,136 sq. ft.

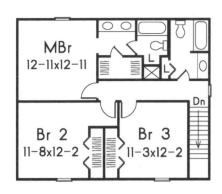

Second Floor
832 sq. ft.

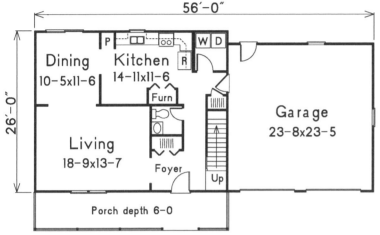

First Floor
832 sq. ft.

Plan #532-001D-0074
Price Code B

Total Living Area: 1,664 Sq. Ft.

Home has 3 bedrooms, 2 1/2 baths, 2-car garage and crawl space foundation, drawings also include basement and slab foundations.

Special features

- L-shaped country kitchen includes pantry and cozy breakfast area
- Bedrooms are located on the second floor for privacy
- Master bedroom includes a walk-in closet, dressing area and bath

LOWE'S

Signature SERIES

Plan #532-041D-0001
Price Code D
Total Living Area: 2,003 Sq. Ft.

Home has 3 bedrooms, 2 baths, 2-car garage and basement foundation.

Special features
- Octagon-shaped dining room with tray ceiling and deck overlook
- L-shaped island kitchen serves living and dining rooms
- Master bedroom boasts luxury bath and walk-in closet
- Living room features columns, elegant fireplace and 10' ceiling

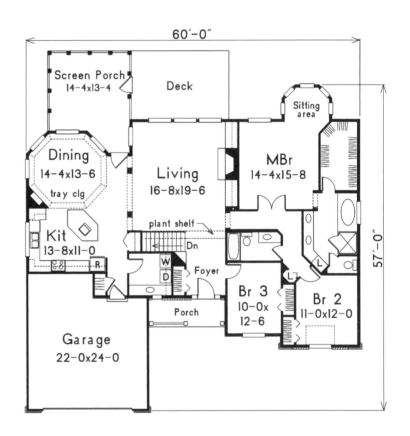

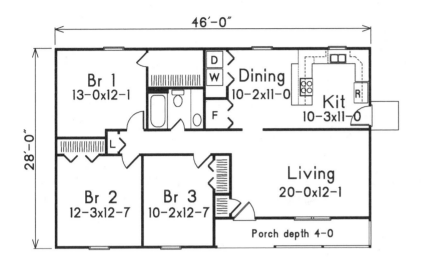

Plan #532-001D-0045
Price Code AA

Total Living Area: 1,197 Sq. Ft.

Home has 3 bedrooms, 1 bath and crawl space foundation, drawings also include basement and slab foundations.

Special features

■ U-shaped kitchen includes ample workspace, breakfast bar, laundry area and direct access to the outdoors

■ Large living room has a convenient coat closet

■ Bedroom #1 features a large walk-in closet

Signature SERIES

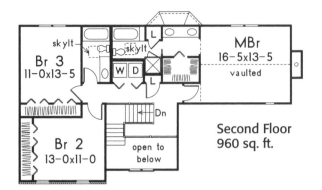

Second Floor
960 sq. ft.

Br 3
11-0x13-5

MBr
16-5x13-5
vaulted

Br 2
13-0x11-0

open to below

Plan #532-003D-0001
Price Code C
Total Living Area: 2,058 Sq. Ft.

Home has 3 bedrooms, 2 1/2 baths, 2-car garage and basement foundation, drawings also include slab and crawl space foundations.

Special features

- Handsome two-story foyer with balcony creates a spacious entrance area

- Vaulted ceiling in the master bedroom with private dressing area and large walk-in closet

- Skylights furnish natural lighting in the hall and master bath

- Laundry closet is conveniently located on the second floor near the bedrooms

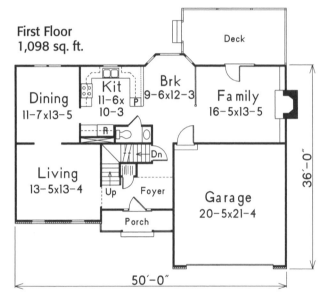

First Floor
1,098 sq. ft.

Deck

Dining
11-7x13-5

Kit
11-6x 10-3

Brk
9-6x12-3

Family
16-5x13-5

Living
13-5x13-4

Up   Foyer   Dn

Garage
20-5x21-4

Porch

36'-0"

50'-0"

Plan #532-001D-0067
Price Code B
Total Living Area: 1,285 Sq. Ft.

Home has 3 bedrooms, 2 baths and crawl space foundation, drawings also include basement and slab foundations.

Special features
- ■ Accommodating home with ranch-style porch
- ■ Large storage area on back of home
- ■ Master bedroom includes dressing area, private bath and built-in bookcase
- ■ Kitchen features pantry, breakfast bar and complete view to the dining room

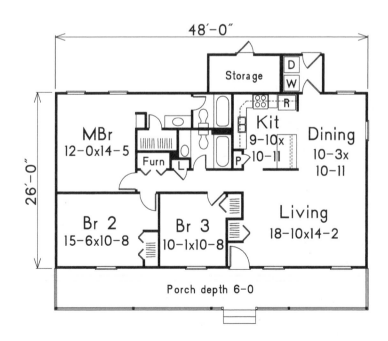

Plan #532-007D-0105
Price Code AA

Total Living Area: 1,084 Sq. Ft.

Home has 2 bedrooms, 2 baths and basement foundation.

Special features
- Delightful country porch for quiet evenings
- The living room offers a front feature window which invites the sun and includes a fireplace and dining area with private patio
- The U-shaped kitchen features lots of cabinets and bayed breakfast room with built-in pantry
- Both bedrooms have walk-in closets and access to their own bath

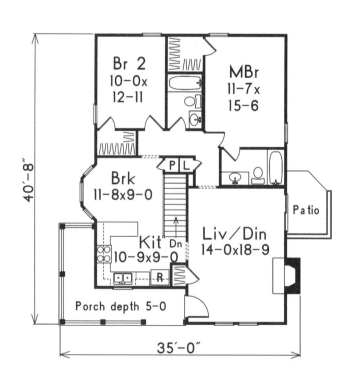

Plan #532-007D-0014
Price Code C

Total Living Area: 1,985 Sq. Ft.

Home has 4 bedrooms, 3 1/2 baths, 2-car garage and basement foundation.

Special features

- ■ Charming design for a narrow lot
- ■ Dramatic sunken great room features vaulted ceiling, large double-hung windows and transomed patio doors
- ■ Grand master bedroom includes a double-door entry, large closet, elegant bath and patio access

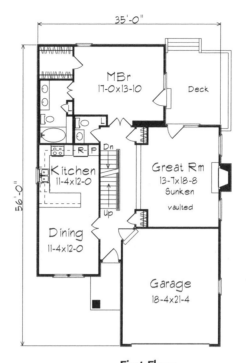

First Floor
1,114 sq. ft.

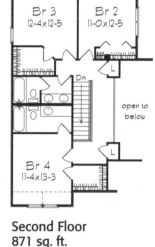

Second Floor
871 sq. ft.

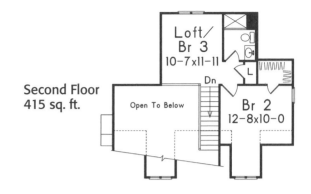

Second Floor
415 sq. ft.

Loft/
Br 3
10-7x11-11

Open To Below

Dn

Br 2
12-8x10-0

Plan #532-058D-0020
Price Code A

Total Living Area: 1,428 Sq. Ft.

Home has 3 bedrooms, 2 baths and basement foundation.

Special features

■ Large vaulted family room opens to dining area and kitchen with breakfast bar

■ First floor master bedroom offers large bath, walk-in closet and nearby laundry facilities

■ A spacious loft/bedroom #3 overlooking the family room and an additional bedroom and bath complement the second floor

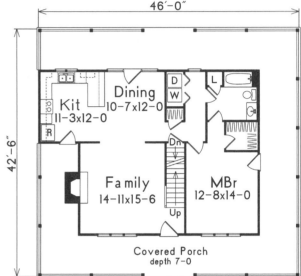

46'-0"

42'-6"

Kit
11-3x12-0

Dining
10-7x12-0

Family
14-11x15-6

MBr
12-8x14-0

Dn

Up

Covered Porch
depth 7-0

First Floor
1,013 sq. ft.

Dormers Accent Country Home

Plan #532-053D-0058
Price Code C
Total Living Area: 1,818 Sq. Ft.

Home has 4 bedrooms, 2 1/2 baths, 2-car drive under garage and basement foundation.

Special features

- Breakfast room is tucked behind the kitchen and has laundry closet and deck access

- Living and dining areas share vaulted ceiling and fireplace

- Master bedroom has two closets, large double-bowl vanity, separate tub and shower

- Large front porch wraps around home

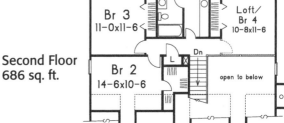

Second Floor
686 sq. ft.

Br 3
11-0x11-6

Loft/
Br 4
10-8x11-6

Dn

Br 2
14-6x10-6

open to below

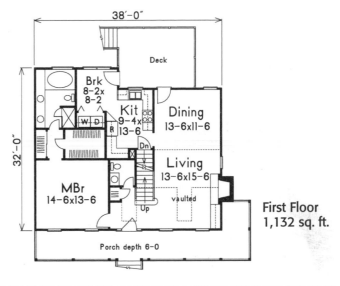

38'-0"

32'-0"

Deck

Brk
8-2x
8-2

Kit
9-4x
13-6

Dining
13-6x11-6

W D

R

Dn

MBr
14-6x13-6

Living
13-6x15-6

vaulted

Up

Porch depth 6-0

First Floor
1,132 sq. ft.

LOWE'S
Signature SERIES

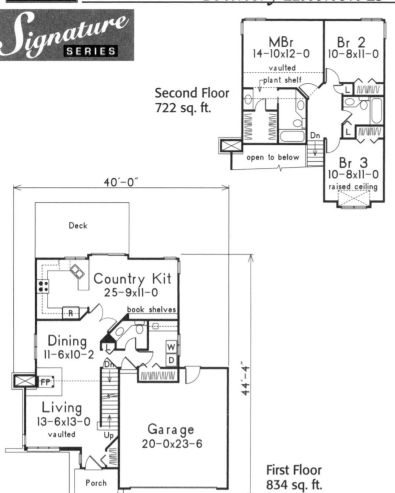

Second Floor
722 sq. ft.

MBr
14-10x12-0
vaulted
plant shelf

Br 2
10-8x11-0

open to below

Dn

Br 3
10-8x11-0
raised ceiling

40'-0"

Deck

Country Kit
25-9x11-0
book shelves

Dining
11-6x10-2

Living
13-6x13-0
vaulted

FP

W
D

Dn

Up

Garage
20-0x23-6

44'-4"

Porch

First Floor
834 sq. ft.

Plan #532-022D-0014
Price Code B
Total Living Area: 1,556 Sq. Ft.

Home has 3 bedrooms, 2 1/2 baths, 2-car garage and basement foundation.

Special features
- A compact home with all the amenities
- Country kitchen combines practicality with access to other areas for eating and entertaining
- Two-way fireplace joins the dining and living areas
- Plant shelf and vaulted ceiling highlight the master bedroom

Lowe's _Signature_ SERIES

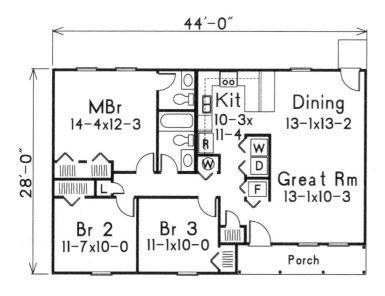

44'-0"

28'-0"

MBr
14-4x12-3

Kit
10-3x
11-4

Dining
13-1x13-2

W
D
F

Great Rm
13-1x10-3

Br 2
11-7x10-0

Br 3
11-1x10-0

Porch

Plan #532-001D-0081
Price Code AA
Total Living Area: 1,160 Sq. Ft.

Home has 3 bedrooms, 1 1/2 baths and crawl space foundation, drawings also include basement and slab foundations.

Special features
- U-shaped kitchen includes breakfast bar and convenient laundry area
- Master bedroom features private half bath and large closet
- Dining room has outdoor access
- Dining and great rooms combine to create an open living atmosphere

Plan #532-058D-0013
Price Code AA

Total Living Area: 1,073 Sq. Ft.

Home has 2 bedrooms, 1 bath and crawl space foundation.

Special features

- Home includes lovely covered front porch and a screened porch off dining area

- Attractive box window brightens kitchen

- Space for efficiency washer and dryer located conveniently between bedrooms

- Family room spotlighted by fireplace with flanking bookshelves and spacious vaulted ceiling

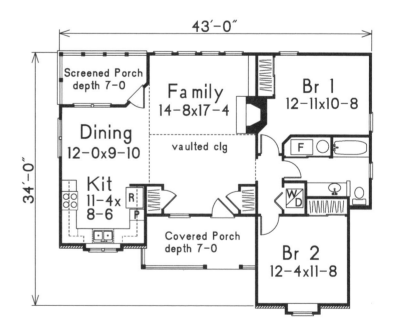

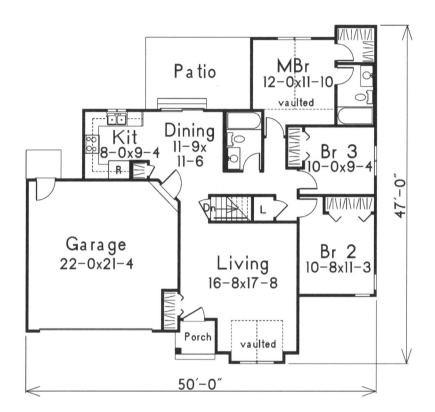

Patio

MBr
12-0x11-10
vaulted

Kit
8-0x9-4

Dining
11-9x
11-6

Br 3
10-0x9-4

R

Dn   L

Garage
22-0x21-4

Living
16-8x17-8

Br 2
10-8x11-3

Porch   vaulted

47'-0"

50'-0"

Plan #532-041D-0004
Price Code AA

Total Living Area: 1,195 Sq. Ft.

Home has 3 bedrooms, 2 baths, 2-car garage and basement foundation.

Special features

■ Dining room opens onto the patio

■ Master bedroom features a vaulted ceiling, private bath and walk-in closet

■ Coat closets are located by both the entrances

■ Convenient secondary entrance is at the back of the garage

LOWE'S

Signature SERIES

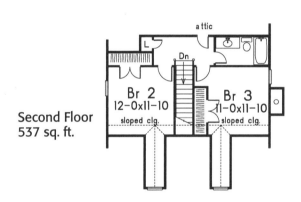

Second Floor
537 sq. ft.

attic

L

Dn

Br 2
12-0x11-10
sloped clg.

Br 3
11-0x11-10
sloped clg.

Plan #532-023D-0016
Price Code B

Total Living Area: 1,609 Sq. Ft.

Home has 3 bedrooms, 2 1/2 baths, 2-car garage and slab foundation.

Special features

- Kitchen captures full use of space with pantry, ample cabinets and workspace
- Master bedroom is well-secluded with a walk-in closet and private bath
- Large utility room includes a sink and extra storage
- Attractive bay window in the dining area provides light

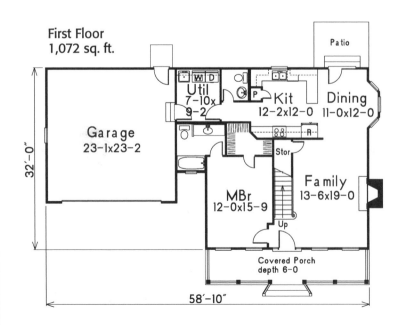

First Floor
1,072 sq. ft.

Patio

W D

Util
7-10x
9-2

Kit
12-2x12-0

Dining
11-0x12-0

P

Garage
23-1x23-2

Stor

R

32'-0"

MBr
12-0x15-9

Family
13-6x19-0

Up

Covered Porch
depth 6-0

58'-10"

LOWE'S
Signature SERIES

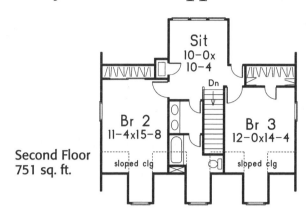

Sit
10-0x
10-4

Br 2
11-4x15-8

Dn

Br 3
12-0x14-4

Second Floor
751 sq. ft.

sloped clg   sloped clg

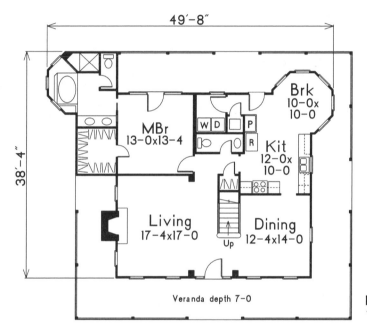

49'-8"

38'-4"

MBr
13-0x13-4

W D

P
R

Brk
10-0x
10-0

Kit
12-0x
10-0

Living
17-4x17-0

Up

Dining
12-4x14-0

Veranda depth 7-0

First Floor
1,308 sq. ft.

Plan #532-037D-0009
Price Code C

Total Living Area: 2,059 Sq. Ft.

Home has 3 bedrooms, 2 1/2 baths,
2-car detached garage and slab foundation, drawings also include basement
and crawl space foundations.

Special features

- Octagon-shaped breakfast room
  offers plenty of windows and
  creates a view to the veranda
- First floor master bedroom has large
  walk-in closet and deluxe bath
- 9' ceilings throughout the home
- Secondary bedrooms and bath
  feature dormers and are adjacent
  to cozy sitting area

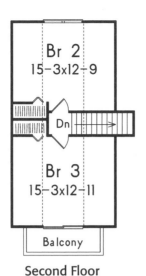

Br 2
15-3x12-9

Dn

Br 3
15-3x12-11

Balcony

Second Floor
450 sq. ft.

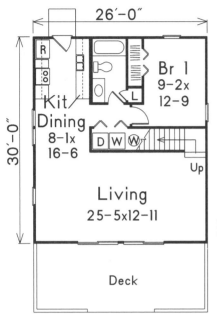

26'-0"

R

Kit
Dining
8-1x
16-6

Br 1
9-2x
12-9

D W W

Up

Living
25-5x12-11

First Floor
780 sq. ft.

30'-0"

Deck

Plan #532-001D-0087
Price Code A

Total Living Area: 1,230 Sq. Ft.

Home has 3 bedrooms, 1 bath and crawl space foundation, drawings also include slab foundation.

Special features
- Spacious living room accesses huge deck
- Bedroom #3 features a balcony overlooking the deck
- Kitchen with dining area accesses the outdoors
- Washer and dryer are tucked under the stairs for space efficiency

Compact Home Is Charming And Functional

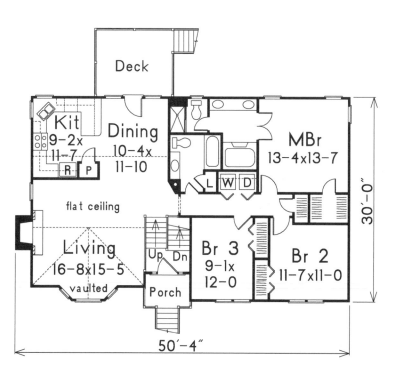

Deck

Kit
9-2x
11-7

Dining
10-4x
11-10

MBr
13-4x13-7

R P

flat ceiling

L W D

Living
16-8x15-5
vaulted

Up Dn

Br 3
9-1x
12-0

Br 2
11-7x11-0

Porch

30'-0"

50'-4"

Plan #532-053D-0032
Price Code A

Total Living Area: 1,404 Sq. Ft.

Home has 3 bedrooms, 2 baths, 2-car drive under garage and basement foundation, drawings also include partial crawl space foundation.

Special features
- Split-foyer entrance
- Bayed living area features a unique vaulted ceiling and fireplace
- Wrap-around kitchen has corner windows for added sunlight and a bar that overlooks dining area
- Master bath features a garden tub with separate shower
- Rear deck provides handy access to dining room and kitchen

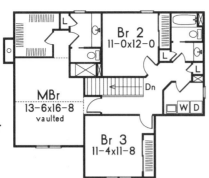

Second Floor
1,016 sq. ft.

Br 2
11-0x12-0

MBr
13-6x16-8
vaulted

Br 3
11-4x11-8

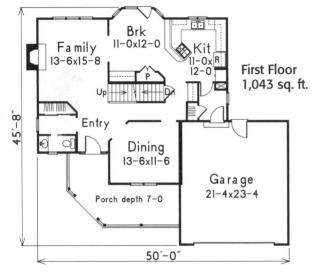

First Floor
1,043 sq. ft.

Family
13-6x15-8

Brk
11-0x12-0

Kit
11-0x
12-0

Entry

Dining
13-6x11-6

Garage
21-4x23-4

Porch depth 7-0

45'-8"

50'-0"

Plan #532-058D-0002
Price Code C

Total Living Area: 2,059 Sq. Ft.

Home has 3 bedrooms, 2 1/2 baths, 2-car garage and basement foundation.

Special features

- Large desk and pantry add to the breakfast room
- Laundry is located on second floor near bedrooms
- Vaulted ceiling in the master bed-room
- Mud room is conveniently located near garage

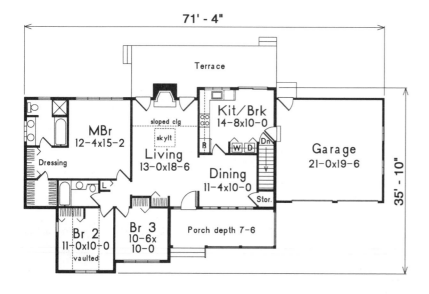

Plan #532-017D-0005
Price Code B
Total Living Area: 1,367 Sq. Ft.

Home has 3 bedrooms, 2 baths, 2-car garage and basement foundation, drawings also include slab foundation.

Special features
- Neat front porch shelters the entrance
- Dining room has full wall of windows and convenient storage area
- Breakfast area leads to the rear terrace through sliding doors
- Large living room with high ceiling, skylight and fireplace

Plan #532-010D-0006
Price Code AA

Total Living Area: 1,170 Sq. Ft.

Home has 3 bedrooms, 2 baths, 2-car garage and slab foundation.

Special features

■ Master bedroom enjoys privacy at the rear of this home

■ Kitchen has an angled bar that overlooks the great room and breakfast area

■ Living areas combine to create a greater sense of spaciousness

■ Great room has a cozy fireplace

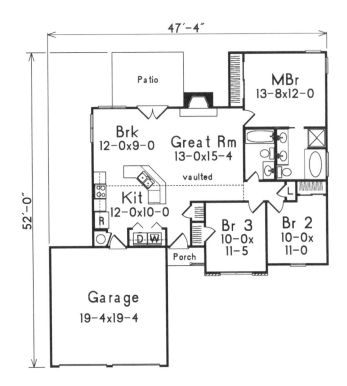

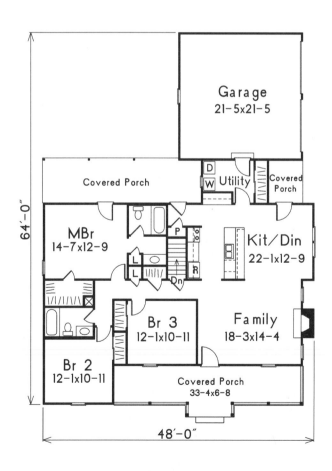

Garage
21-5x21-5

Covered Porch

D
W Utility

Covered Porch

MBr
14-7x12-9

Kit/Din
22-1x12-9

P

L
L

Dn

64'-0"

Br 3
12-1x10-11

Family
18-3x14-4

Br 2
12-1x10-11

Covered Porch
33-4x6-8

48'-0"

Plan #532-001D-0031
Price Code B
Total Living Area: 1,501 Sq. Ft.

Home has 3 bedrooms, 2 baths, 2-car side entry garage and basement foundation, drawings also include crawl space and slab foundations.

Special features
- Spacious kitchen with dining area is open to the outdoors
- Convenient utility room is adjacent to garage
- Master bedroom features a private bath, dressing area and access to the large covered porch
- Large family room creates openness

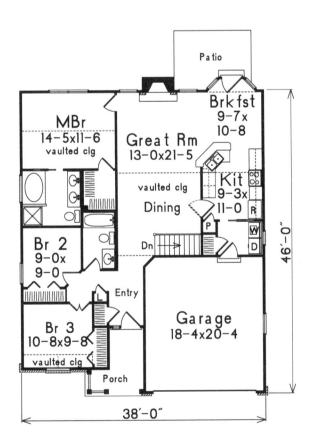

Plan #532-007D-0060
Price Code B
Total Living Area: 1,268 Sq. Ft.

Home has 3 bedrooms, 2 baths, 2-car garage and basement foundation, drawings also include slab and crawl space foundations.

Special features
- Multiple gables, large porch and arched windows create a classy exterior
- Innovative design provides openness in great room, kitchen and breakfast room
- Secondary bedrooms have private hall with bath

LOWE'S

Signature SERIES

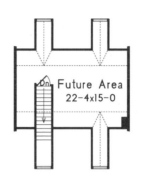

Optional Second Floor

Future Area 22-4x15-0

Plan #532-017D-0007
Price Code C

Total Living Area: 1,567 Sq. Ft.

Home has 3 bedrooms, 2 baths, 2-car side entry garage and partial basement/crawl space foundation, drawings also include slab foundation.

Special features

- Living room flows into the dining room shaped by an angled pass-through into the kitchen

- Cheerful, windowed dining area

- Future area available on the second floor has an additional 338 square feet of living area

- Master bedroom is separated from other bedrooms for privacy

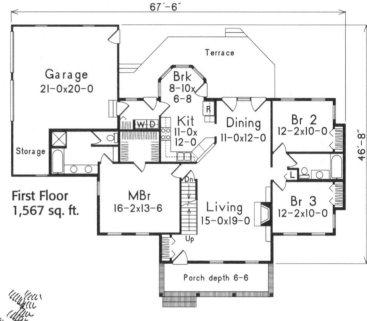

67'-6"

Garage 21-0x20-0

Terrace

Brk 8-10x 6-8

Storage

W D

Kit 11-0x 12-0

R

Dining 11-0x12-0

Br 2 12-2x10-0

46'-8"

First Floor 1,567 sq. ft.

MBr 16-2x13-6

Living 15-0x19-0

Br 3 12-2x10-0

Up

Porch depth 6-6

FGURNIER INC. NAG

Plan #532-001D-0013
Price Code D

Total Living Area: 1,882 Sq. Ft.

Home has 3 bedrooms, 2 baths, 2-car garage and basement foundation.

Special features

■ Wide, handsome entrance opens to the vaulted great room with fire-place

■ Living and dining areas are conveniently joined but still allow privacy

■ Private covered porch extends breakfast area

■ Practical passageway runs through the laundry and mud room from the garage to the kitchen

■ Vaulted ceiling in master bedroom

Plan #532-001D-0035
Price Code A

Total Living Area: 1,396 Sq. Ft.

Home has 3 bedrooms, 2 baths, 1-car carport and basement foundation, drawings also include crawl space foundation.

Special features

- Gabled front adds interest to facade
- Living and dining rooms share a vaulted ceiling
- Master bedroom features a walk-in closet and private bath
- Functional kitchen boasts a center work island and convenient pantry

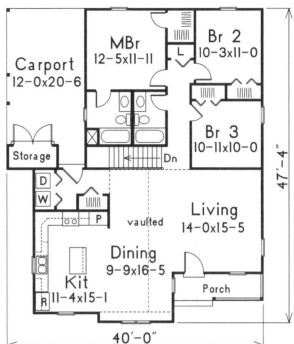

Plan #532-040D-0026
Price Code B
Total Living Area: 1,393 Sq. Ft.

Home has 3 bedrooms, 2 baths, 2-car detached garage and crawl space foundation, drawings also include slab foundation.

Special features

- ■ L-shaped kitchen features a walk-in pantry, island cooktop and is convenient to laundry room and dining area

- ■ Master bedroom features a large walk-in closet and private bath with separate tub and shower

- ■ Convenient storage/coat closet in hall

- ■ View to the patio from the dining area

Plan #532-023D-0018
Price Code B

Total Living Area: 1,556 Sq. Ft.

Home has 3 bedrooms, 2 baths, 2-car attached carport and slab foundation.

Special features

- Corner fireplace in the living area warms surroundings
- Spacious master bedroom includes a walk-in closet and private bath with double-bowl vanity
- Compact kitchen is designed for efficiency
- Covered porches in both front and back of home add coziness

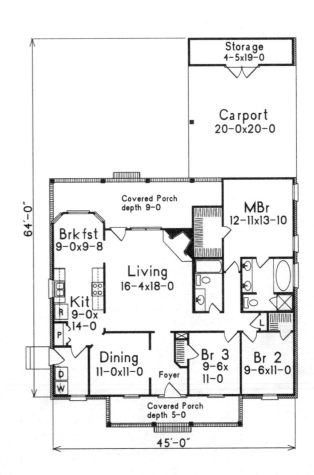

Storage
4-5x19-0

Carport
20-0x20-0

64'-0"

Covered Porch
depth 9-0

MBr
12-11x13-10

Brkfst
9-0x9-8

Living
16-4x18-0

Kit
9-0x
14-0

Dining
11-0x11-0

Foyer

Br 3
9-6x
11-0

Br 2
9-6x11-0

Covered Porch
depth 5-0

45'-0"

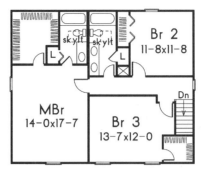

Second Floor
938 sq. ft.

Plan #532-001D-0025
Price Code D

Total Living Area: 1,998 Sq. Ft.

Home has 3 bedrooms, 2 1/2 baths, 2-car side entry garage and basement foundation, drawings also include crawl space and slab foundations.

Special features

- Large family room features a fireplace and access to the kitchen and dining area
- Skylights add daylight to the second floor baths
- Utility room is conveniently located near the garage and kitchen
- Kitchen/breakfast area includes a pantry, island workspace and easy access to the patio

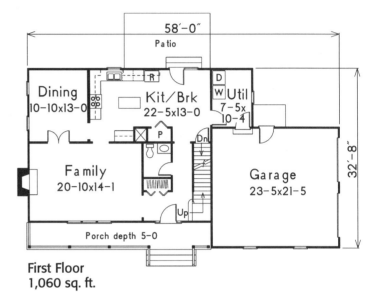

First Floor
1,060 sq. ft.

Plan #532-007D-0035
Price Code B

Total Living Area: 1,619 Sq. Ft.

Home has 3 bedrooms, 2 1/2 baths, 2-car side entry garage and basement foundation.

Special features

- Elegant home features three quaint porches and a large rear patio
- Grand-scale great room offers a dining area, fireplace with a built-in alcove and shelves for an entertainment center
- First floor master bedroom has a walk-in closet, luxury bath, bay window and access to rear patio
- Breakfast room with bay window contains a staircase that leads to the second floor bedrooms and loft

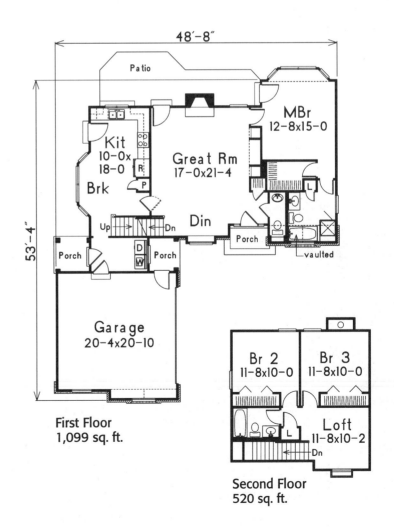

First Floor
1,099 sq. ft.

Second Floor
520 sq. ft.

SPARR

Plan #532-001D-0058
Price Code B
Total Living Area: 1,720 Sq. Ft.

Home has 3 bedrooms, 1 full bath, 2 half baths, 2-car drive under garage and basement foundation.

Special features
- Lower level includes large family room with laundry area and half bath
- L-shaped kitchen has a convenient serving bar and pass-through to dining area
- Private half bath in master bedroom

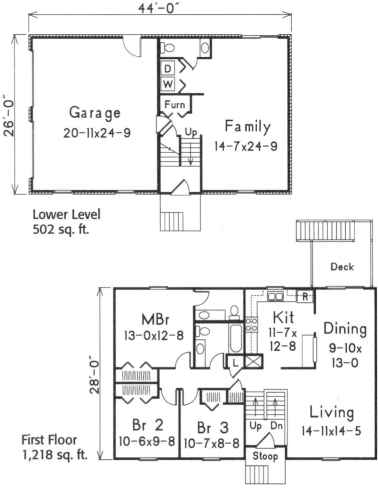

44'-0"

26'-0"

Garage
20-11x24-9

D
W

Furn

Up

Family
14-7x24-9

Lower Level
502 sq. ft.

Deck

MBr
13-0x12-8

Kit
11-7x
12-8

Dining
9-10x
13-0

L

R

28'-0"

Br 2
10-6x9-8

Br 3
10-7x8-8

Up Dn

Living
14-11x14-5

First Floor
1,218 sq. ft.

Stoop

Plan #532-058D-0016
Price Code B
Total Living Area: 1,558 Sq. Ft.

Home has 3 bedrooms, 2 baths, 2-car garage and basement foundation.

Special features

■ The spacious utility room is located conveniently between the garage and kitchen/dining area

■ Bedrooms are separated from the living area by hallway

■ Enormous living area with fireplace and vaulted ceiling opens to the kitchen and dining area

■ Master bedroom is enhanced with a large bay window, walk-in closet and private bath

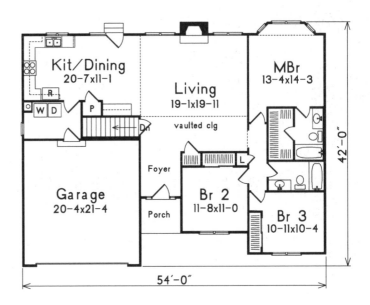

Kit/Dining
20-7x11-1

Living
19-1x19-11
vaulted clg

MBr
13-4x14-3

Garage
20-4x21-4

Foyer

Br 2
11-8x11-0

Br 3
10-11x10-4

Porch

42'-0"

54'-0"

Plan #532-040D-0015
Price Code B

Total Living Area: 1,655 Sq. Ft.

Home has 3 bedrooms, 2 baths, 2-car garage and crawl space foundation.

Special features

- Master bedroom features a 9' ceiling, walk-in closet and bath with dressing area
- Oversized family room includes 10' ceiling and masonry see-through fireplace
- Island kitchen with convenient access to laundry room
- Handy covered walkway from garage to kitchen and dining area

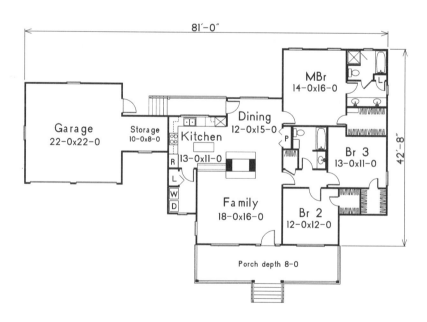

Distinctive Home For Sloping Terrain

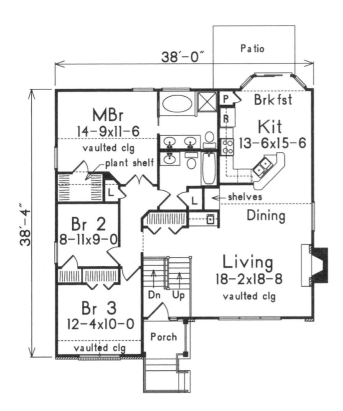

Plan #532-007D-0061
Price Code A

Total Living Area: 1,340 Sq. Ft.

Home has 3 bedrooms, 2 baths, 2-car drive under garage with storage area and basement foundation.

Special features

- Grand-sized vaulted living and dining rooms offer fireplace, wet bar and breakfast counter open to spacious kitchen

- Vaulted master bedroom features a double-door entry, walk-in closet and an elegant bath

- Basement includes a huge two-car garage and space for a bedroom/bath expansion

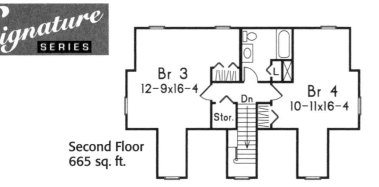

Second Floor
665 sq. ft.

Br 3
12-9x16-4

Br 4
10-11x16-4

Dn

Stor.

L

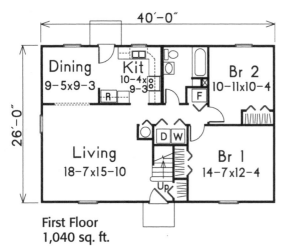

40'-0"

26'-0"

Dining
9-5x9-3

Kit
10-4x
9-3

Br 2
10-11x10-4

R

F

Living
18-7x15-10

D W

Br 1
14-7x12-4

Up

First Floor
1,040 sq. ft.

Plan #532-001D-0056
Price Code B

Total Living Area: 1,705 Sq. Ft.

Home has 4 bedrooms, 2 baths and crawl space foundation, drawings also include basement and slab foundations.

Special features

- Cozy design includes two bedrooms on first floor and two bedrooms on second floor for added privacy
- L-shaped kitchen provides easy access to the dining room and the outdoors
- Convenient first floor laundry area

Second Floor
360 sq. ft.

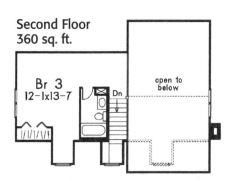

Br 3
12-1x13-7

open to below

Dn

Plan #532-029D-0002
Price Code B

Total Living Area: 1,619 Sq. Ft.

Home has 3 bedrooms, 3 baths and basement foundation, drawings also include crawl space and slab foundations.

Special features

- Private second floor bedroom and bath
- Kitchen features a snack bar and adjacent dining area
- Master bedroom has a private bath
- Centrally located washer and dryer

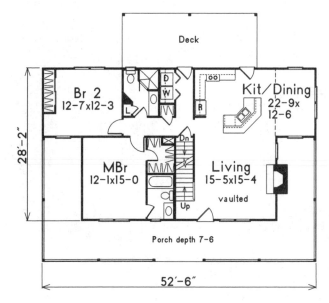

Deck

Br 2
12-7x12-3

Kit/Dining
22-9x
12-6

28'-2"

MBr
12-1x15-0

Living
15-5x15-4
vaulted

Dn

Up

Porch depth 7-6

First Floor
1,259 sq. ft.

52'-6"

Plan #532-058D-0012
Price Code AA

Total Living Area: 1,143 Sq. Ft.

Home has 2 bedrooms, 1 bath and crawl space foundation.

Special features

- Enormous stone fireplace in family room adds warmth and character
- Spacious kitchen with breakfast bar overlooks family room
- Separate dining area is great for entertaining
- Vaulted family room and kitchen create an open atmosphere

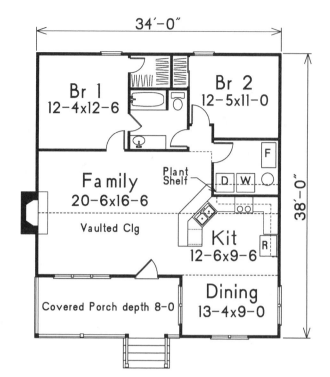

34'-0"

Br 1
12-4x12-6

Br 2
12-5x11-0

Family
20-6x16-6

Plant Shelf

F

D W

Vaulted Clg

Kit
12-6x9-6

R

38'-0"

Covered Porch depth 8-0

Dining
13-4x9-0

LOWE'S
Signature SERIES

Plan #532-053D-0029
Price Code A
Total Living Area: 1,220 Sq. Ft.

Home has 3 bedrooms, 2 baths, 2-car drive under garage and basement foundation.

Special features

- Vaulted ceilings add luxury to the living room and master bedroom
- Spacious living room is accented with a large fireplace and hearth
- Gracious dining area is adjacent to the convenient wrap-around kitchen
- Washer and dryer are handy to the bedrooms
- Covered porch entry adds appeal
- Rear deck adjoins dining area

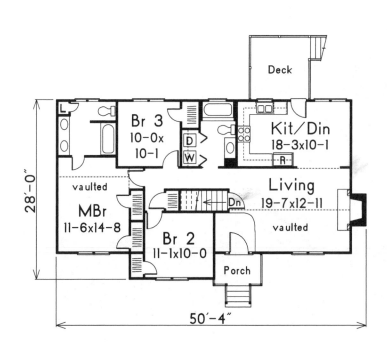

Upscale Ranch With Formal And Informal Areas

Plan #532-068D-0004
Price Code C
Total Living Area: 1,969 Sq. Ft.

Home has 3 bedrooms, 2 baths, 2-car garage and crawl space foundation, drawings also include slab foundation.

Special features
- Master bedroom boasts a luxurious bath with double sinks, two walk-in closets and an oversized tub
- Corner fireplace warms a conveniently located family area
- Formal living and dining areas in the front of the home lend a touch of privacy when entertaining
- Spacious utility room has counterspace and a sink

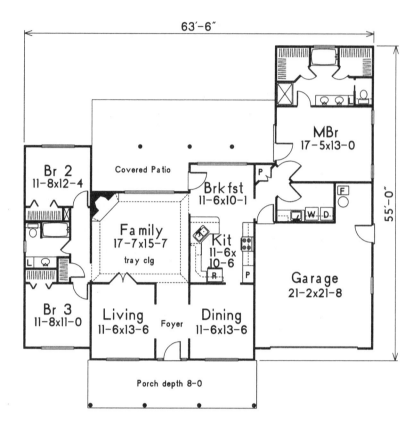

63'-6"

55'-0"

MBr
17-5x13-0

Br 2
11-8x12-4

Covered Patio

Brkfst
11-6x10-1

Family
17-7x15-7
tray clg

Kit
11-6x
10-6

Garage
21-2x21-8

Br 3
11-8x11-0

Living
11-6x13-6

Foyer

Dining
11-6x13-6

Porch depth 8-0

English Cottage With Modern Amenities

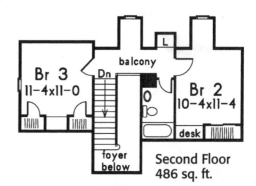

Plan #532-037D-0002
Price Code C
Total Living Area: 1,816 Sq. Ft.

Home has 3 bedrooms, 2 1/2 baths, 2-car detached garage and slab foundation, drawings also include crawl space foundation.

Special features

- Two-way living room fireplace with large nearby window seat
- Wrap-around dining room windows create sunroom appearance
- Master bedroom has abundant closet and storage space
- Rear dormers, closets and desk areas create an interesting and functional second floor

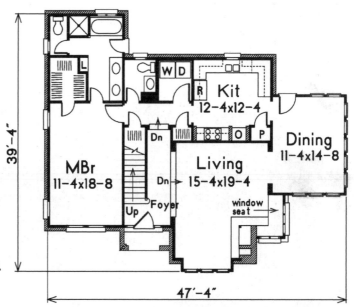

LOWE'S
Signature **SERIES**

Plan #532-008D-0045
Price Code B

Total Living Area: 1,540 Sq. Ft.

Home has 3 bedrooms, 2 baths, 2-car garage and basement foundation, drawings also include crawl space and slab foundations.

Special features

- Porch entrance into foyer leads to an impressive dining area with full window and a half-circle window above

- Kitchen/breakfast room features a center island and cathedral ceiling

- Great room with cathedral ceiling and exposed beams is accessible from foyer

- Master bedroom includes full bath and walk-in closet

- Two additional bedrooms share a full bath

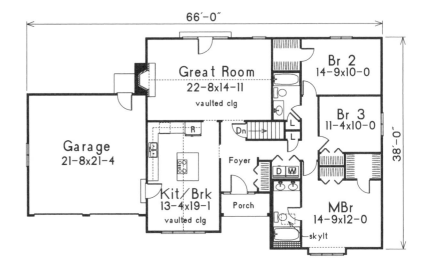

Plan #532-058D-0006
Price Code A
Total Living Area: 1,339 Sq. Ft.

Home has 3 bedrooms, 2 1/2 baths and crawl space foundation.

Special features

- Full-length covered porch enhances front facade

- Vaulted ceiling and stone fireplace add drama to family room

- Walk-in closets in bedrooms provide ample storage space

- Combined kitchen/dining area adjoins family room for the perfect entertaining space

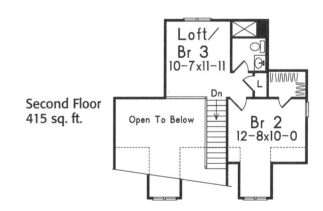

Second Floor
415 sq. ft.

Loft/Br 3
10-7x11-11

Open To Below

Dn

L

Br 2
12-8x10-0

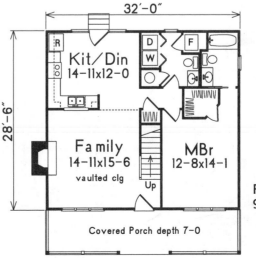

32'-0"

28'-6"

R

Kit/Din
14-11x12-0

D W F

Family
14-11x15-6
vaulted clg

Up

MBr
12-8x14-1

First Floor
924 sq. ft.

Covered Porch depth 7-0

Second Floor
615 sq. ft.

Plan #532-040D-0027
Price Code C
Total Living Area: 1,597 Sq. Ft.

Home has 4 bedrooms, 2 1/2 baths, 2-car detached garage and basement foundation.

Special features

- ■ Spacious family room includes fireplace and coat closet

- ■ Open kitchen and dining room provide breakfast bar and access to the outdoors

- ■ Convenient laundry area is located near kitchen

- ■ Secluded master bedroom with walk-in closet and private bath

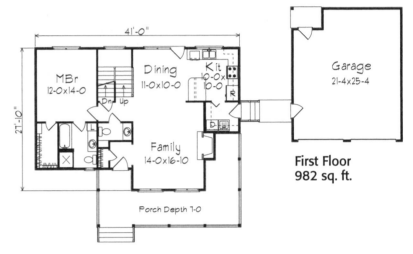

First Floor
982 sq. ft.

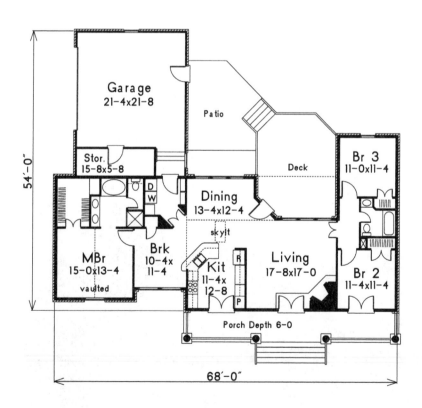

Plan #532-021D-0012
Price Code C

Total Living Area: 1,672 Sq. Ft.

Home has 3 bedrooms, 2 baths, 2-car side entry garage and crawl space foundation, drawings also include basement and slab foundations.

Special features

- Vaulted master bedroom features a walk-in closet and adjoining bath with separate tub and shower
- Energy efficient home with 2" x 6" exterior walls
- Covered front and rear porches
- 12' ceilings in living room, kitchen and bedroom #2
- Kitchen is complete with a pantry, angled bar and adjacent eating area
- Sloped ceiling in dining room

LOWE'S

Signature **SERIES**

Plan #532-058D-0021
Price Code A
Total Living Area: 1,477 Sq. Ft.

Home has 3 bedrooms, 2 baths, 2-car side entry garage with storage area and basement foundation.

Special features

- Oversized porch provides protection from the elements
- Innovative kitchen employs step-saving design
- Kitchen has snack bar which opens to the breakfast room with bay window

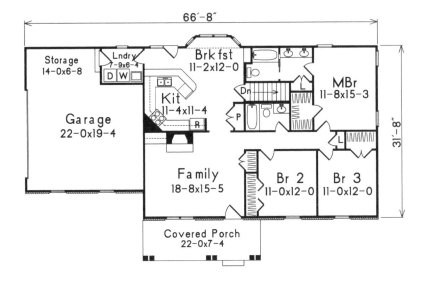

66'-8"

Storage 14-0x6-8

Lndry 7-9x6-4

Brkfst 11-2x12-0

MBr 11-8x15-3

31'-8"

Garage 22-0x19-4

Kit 11-4x11-4

Family 18-8x15-5

Br 2 11-0x12-0

Br 3 11-0x12-0

Covered Porch 22-0x7-4

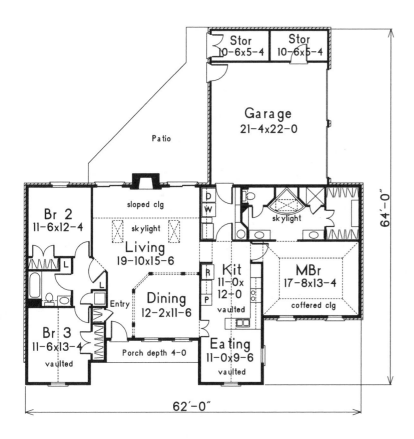

Stor 10-6x5-4

Stor 10-6x5-4

Garage 21-4x22-0

Patio

64'-0"

sloped clg

skylight

Br 2 11-6x12-4

Living 19-10x15-6

L

Entry

Dining 12-2x11-6

D

W

R

P

Kit 11-0x 12-0 vaulted

skylight

MBr 17-8x13-4

coffered clg

Br 3 11-6x13-4 vaulted

Porch depth 4-0

Eating 11-0x9-6 vaulted

62'-0"

Plan #532-021D-0007
Price Code D

Total Living Area: 1,868 Sq. Ft.

Home has 3 bedrooms, 2 baths, 2-car side entry garage and slab foundation, drawings also include crawl space foundation.

Special features

- Luxurious master bath is impressive with an angled quarter-circle tub, separate vanities and large walk-in closet
- Energy efficient home with 2" x 6" exterior walls
- Dining room is surrounded by a series of arched openings which complement the open feeling of this design
- Living room has a 12' ceiling accented by skylights and a large fireplace flanked by sliding doors
- Large storage areas

Plan #532-007D-0085
Price Code B

Total Living Area: 1,787 Sq. Ft.

Home has 3 bedrooms, 2 baths, 2-car drive under garage and walk-out basement foundation.

Special features

■ Large great room with fireplace and vaulted ceiling features three large skylights and windows galore

■ Cooking is sure to be a pleasure in this L-shaped well-appointed kitchen which includes bayed breakfast area with access to rear deck

■ Every bedroom offers a spacious walk-in closet with a convenient laundry room just steps away

■ 415 square feet of optional living area available on the lower level

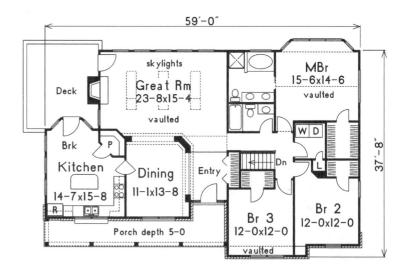

LOWE'S

Signature SERIES

Plan #532-007D-0045
Price Code A

Total Living Area: 1,321 Sq. Ft.

Home has 3 bedrooms, 2 baths, 1-car rear entry garage and basement foundation.

Special features

- Rear entry garage and elongated brick wall add to appealing facade
- Dramatic vaulted living room includes corner fireplace and towering feature windows
- Breakfast room is immersed in light from two large windows and glass sliding doors

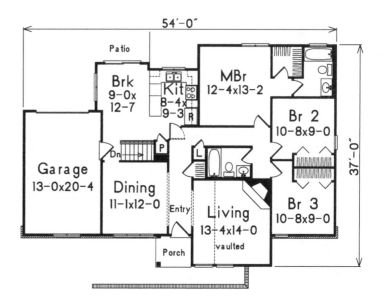

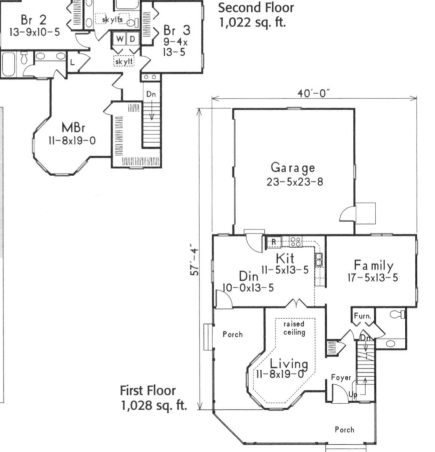

Second Floor
1,022 sq. ft.

Br 2
13-9x10-5

skylts

W D

Br 3
9-4x
13-5

skylt

L

Dn

MBr
11-8x19-0

Plan #532-001D-0059

Price Code C

Total Living Area:	2,050 Sq. Ft.

Home has 3 bedrooms, 2 1/2 baths, 2-car side entry garage and basement foundation, drawings also include crawl space and slab foundations.

Special features

- Large kitchen and dining area have access to garage and porch
- Master bedroom features a unique turret design, private bath and large walk-in closet
- Laundry facilities are conveniently located near the bedrooms

40'-0"

57'-4"

Garage
23-5x23-8

Kit
11-5x13-5

Din
10-0x13-5

Family
17-5x13-5

R

Furn.

raised ceiling

Porch

Living
11-8x19-0

Foyer

Up

First Floor
1,028 sq. ft.

Porch

LOWE'S

Signature SERIES

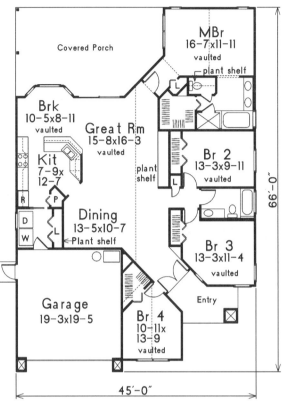

Covered Porch

MBr
16-7x11-11
vaulted

plant shelf

Brk
10-5x8-11
vaulted

Great Rm
15-8x16-3
vaulted

Kit
7-9x
12-7

plant shelf

Br 2
13-3x9-11
vaulted

Dining
13-5x10-7
Plant shelf

Br 3
13-3x11-4
vaulted

Garage
19-3x19-5

Br 4
10-11x
13-9
vaulted

Entry

66'-0"

45'-0"

Plan #532-048D-0001
Price Code D
Total Living Area: 1,865 Sq. Ft.

Home has 4 bedrooms, 2 baths, 2-car garage and slab foundation, drawings also include crawl space foundation.

Special features

- The large foyer opens into an expansive dining area and great room
- Home features vaulted ceilings throughout
- Master bedroom features an angled entry, vaulted ceiling, plant shelf and bath with double vanity, tub and shower

Plan #532-008D-0010
Price Code A

Total Living Area: 1,440 Sq. Ft.

Home has 3 bedrooms, 2 baths, 2-car side entry garage and basement foundation, drawings also include crawl space and slab foundations.

Special features

■ Foyer adjoins massive-sized great room with sloping ceiling and tall masonry fireplace

■ The kitchen connects to the spacious dining room and features a pass-through to the breakfast bar

■ Master bedroom enjoys a private bath and two closets

■ An oversized two-car side entry garage offers plenty of storage for bicycles, lawn equipment, etc.

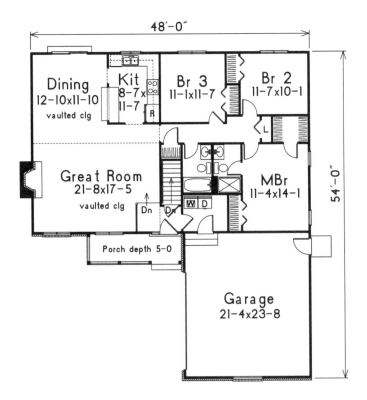

Cottage With Atrium

Optional
Lower Level

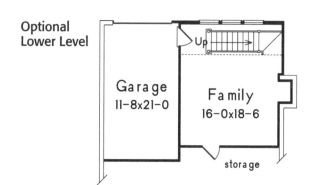

Garage
11-8x21-0

Family
16-0x18-6

storage

Plan #532-007D-0104
Price Code AA

Total Living Area: 969 Sq. Ft.

Home has 2 bedrooms, 1 bath, 1-car rear entry garage and walk-out basement foundation.

Special features

- Eye-pleasing facade enjoys stone accents with country porch for quiet evenings
- A bayed dining area, cozy fireplace and atrium with sunny two-story windows are the many features of the living room
- Step-saver kitchen includes a pass-through snack bar
- 325 square feet of optional living area on the lower level

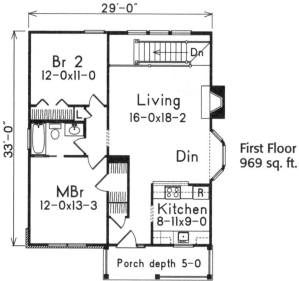

29'-0"

33'-0"

Br 2
12-0x11-0

Living
16-0x18-2

Dn

Din

MBr
12-0x13-3

Kitchen
8-11x9-0

R

First Floor
969 sq. ft.

Porch depth 5-0

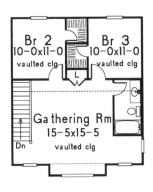

Br 2
10-0x11-0
vaulted clg

Br 3
10-0x11-0
vaulted clg

L

Gathering Rm
15-5x15-5
vaulted clg

Dn

Second Floor
672 sq. ft.

Plan #532-068D-0003
Price Code B

Total Living Area: 1,784 Sq. Ft.

Home has 3 bedrooms, 2 1/2 baths, 1-car garage and basement foundation, drawings also include crawl space foundation.

Special features

- Spacious living area with corner fireplace offers a cheerful atmosphere with large windows

- Large second floor gathering room is great for kid's play area

- Secluded master bedroom has separate porch entrances and a large master bath with walk-in closet

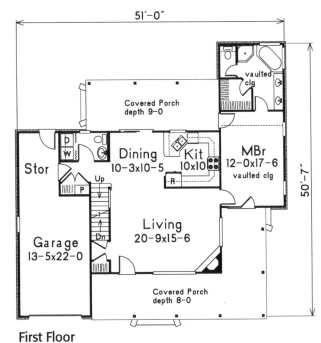

51'-0"

50'-7"

Covered Porch
depth 9-0

vaulted clg

D W

Dining
10-3x10-5

Kit
10x10

MBr
12-0x17-6
vaulted clg

Stor

P

Up

R

Garage
13-5x22-0

Dn

Living
20-9x15-6

Covered Porch
depth 8-0

First Floor
1,112 sq. ft.

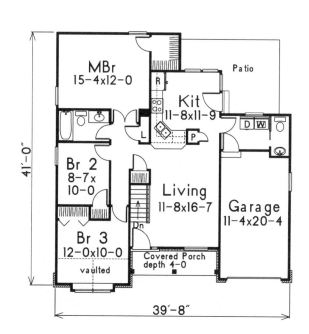

Plan #532-007D-0031
Price Code AA
Total Living Area: 1,092 Sq. Ft.

Home has 3 bedrooms, 1 1/2 baths, 1-car garage and basement foundation.

Special features

■ Box window and inviting porch with dormers create a charming facade

■ Eat-in kitchen offers a pass-through breakfast bar, corner window wall to patio, pantry and convenient laundry with half bath

■ Master bedroom features a double-door entry and walk-in closet

MBr
15-4x12-0

Patio

Kit
11-8x11-9

R

D W

L

P

Br 2
8-7 x
10-0

Living
11-8x16-7

Garage
11-4x20-4

Dn

Br 3
12-0x10-0
vaulted

Covered Porch
depth 4-0

41'-0"

39'-8"

Signature
SERIES

First Floor
996 sq. ft.

Deck

Dining
10-8x12-0
vaulted

Skylts

Dn

plant shelf   vaulted

plant shelf

Kit
10-4x11-4
vaulted

P

Great Room
16-0x15-9

MBr
12-5x15-0

R

46'-8"

Porch

Garage
18-4x20-4

46'-0"

46'-0"

Lower Level
945 sq. ft.

Br 3
9-9x10-4

Atrium
9-6x7-1

Up

Br 2
12-3x11-6

24'-4"

Family
16-0x15-5

Bar

L

Br 4
9-9x10-1

Storage
18-0x9-3

D
W

Plan #532-007D-0018
Price Code C

Total Living Area: 1,941 Sq. Ft.

Home has 4 bedrooms, 2 1/2 baths, 2-car garage and walk-out basement foundation.

Special features

- Dramatic, exciting and spacious interior
- Vaulted great room is brightened by a sunken atrium window wall and skylights
- Vaulted U-shaped gourmet kitchen with plant shelf opens to dining room
- First floor half bath features space for stackable washer and dryer

Garden Courtyard Lends Distinction, Privacy

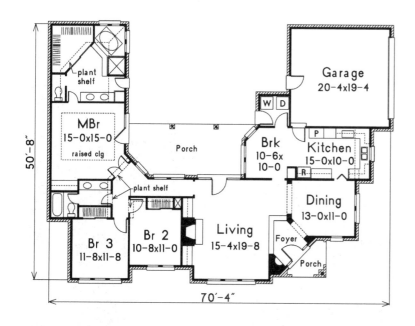

Plan #532-037D-0003
Price Code D

Total Living Area: 1,996 Sq. Ft.

Home has 3 bedrooms, 2 baths, 2-car side entry garage and slab foundation, drawings also include crawl space foundation.

Special features

- Garden courtyard comes with large porch and direct access to master bedroom suite, breakfast room and garage
- Sculptured entrance has artful plant shelves and special niche in foyer
- Master bedroom boasts French doors, garden tub, desk with book-shelves and generous storage
- Plant shelves and high ceilings grace hallway

Exciting Living For A Narrow Sloping Lot

Plan #532-007D-0106
Price Code A

Total Living Area: 1,200 Sq. Ft.

Home has 2 bedrooms, 1 bath and walk-out basement foundation.

Special features

- Entry leads to a large dining area which opens to kitchen and sun-drenched living room
- An expansive window wall in the two-story atrium lends space and light to living room with fireplace
- The large kitchen features a break-fast bar, built-in pantry and storage galore
- 697 square feet of optional living area on the lower level includes a family room, bedroom #3 and a bath

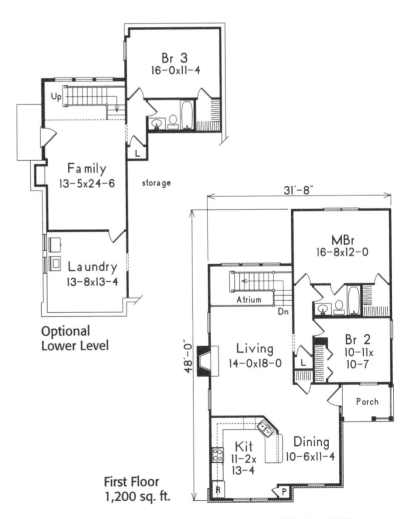

Br 3
16-0x11-4

Up

Family
13-5x24-6

storage

L

Laundry
13-8x13-4

Optional
Lower Level

31'-8"

MBr
16-8x12-0

Atrium
Dn

48'-0"

Living
14-0x18-0

Br 2
10-11x
10-7

L

Porch

Kit
11-2x
13-4

Dining
10-6x11-4

R

P

First Floor
1,200 sq. ft.

Covered Porch Surrounds Home

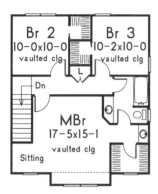

Second Floor
667 sq. ft.

Br 2
10-0x10-0
vaulted clg

Br 3
10-2x10-0
vaulted clg

Dn

MBr
17-5x15-1
vaulted clg

Sitting

First Floor
732 sq. ft.

Opt. 2 Car Garage

Covered Porch depth 8-0

Shop
7-7x
11-9

Dining
10-3x
10-5

Kit
10-6x10-5

Garage
14-0x22-2

Living Rm
20-9x15-6

Dn

Up

Covered Porch depth 8-0

43'-6"

46'-8 1/2"

Plan #532-068D-0006
Price Code A

Total Living Area: 1,399 Sq. Ft.

Home has 3 bedrooms, 1 1/2 baths, 1-car garage and basement foundation, drawings also include crawl space and slab foundations.

Special features

- Living room overlooks dining area through arched columns

- Laundry room contains handy half bath

- Spacious master bedroom includes sitting area, walk-in closet and plenty of sunlight

Signature SERIES

Plan #532-068D-0005
Price Code A

Total Living Area: 1,433 Sq. Ft.

Home has 3 bedrooms, 2 baths, 2-car garage and basement foundation, drawings also include crawl space and slab foundations.

Special features

■ Vaulted living room includes cozy fireplace and an oversized entertainment center

■ Bedrooms #2 and #3 share a full bath

■ Master bedroom has a full bath and large walk-in closet

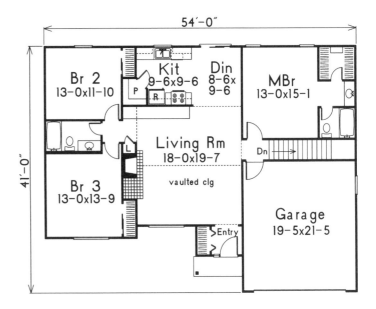

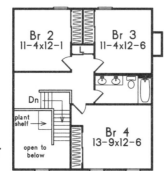

Second Floor
770 sq. ft.

Br 2
11-4x12-1

Br 3
11-4x12-6

Dn

plant shelf

Br 4
13-9x12-6

open to below

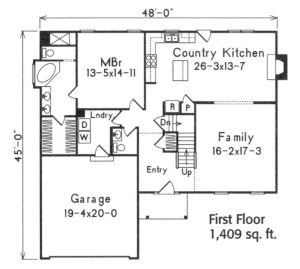

48'-0"

45'-0"

MBr
13-5x14-11

Country Kitchen
26-3x13-7

Lndry

D W

R P
Dn

Family
16-2x17-3

Entry Up

Garage
19-4x20-0

First Floor
1,409 sq. ft.

Plan #532-058D-0037
Price Code C

Total Living Area: 2,179 Sq. Ft.

Home has 4 bedrooms, 2 1/2 baths, 2-car garage and basement foundation.

Special features

■ Open floor plan and minimal halls eliminate wasted space and create efficiency

■ First floor master bedroom is conveniently located near large kitchen

■ Three bedrooms on the second floor share a large bath with nearby linen closet

Plan #532-058D-0029
Price Code AA

Total Living Area: 1,000 Sq. Ft.

Home has 2 bedrooms, 1 bath and crawl space foundation.

Special features

- Large mud room has a separate covered porch entrance
- Full-length covered front porch
- Bedrooms on opposite sides of the home for privacy
- Vaulted ceiling creates an open and spacious feeling

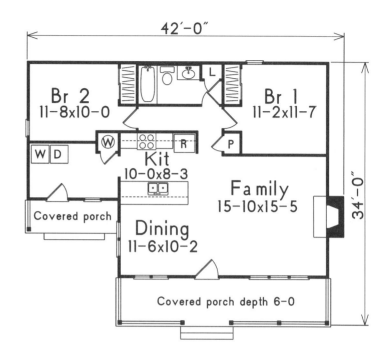

42'-0"

34'-0"

Br 2
11-8x10-0

Br 1
11-2x11-7

W D

Kit
10-0x8-3

Family
15-10x15-5

Covered porch

Dining
11-6x10-2

Covered porch depth 6-0

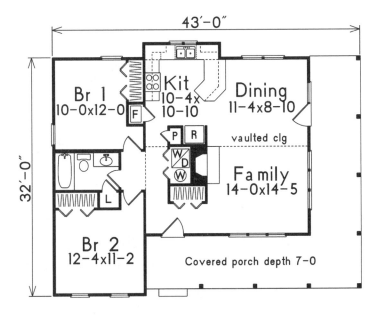

43'-0"

32'-0"

Br 1
10-0x12-0

F

Kit
10-4x
10-10

Dining
11-4x8-10

P R

vaulted clg

W/D
W

Family
14-0x14-5

L

Br 2
12-4x11-2

Covered porch depth 7-0

Plan #532-058D-0030
Price Code AA

Total Living Area: 990 Sq. Ft.

Home has 2 bedrooms, 1 bath and crawl space foundation.

Special features

- Wrap-around porch on two sides of this home

- Covered porch surrounding one side of this home maintains privacy

- Space for efficiency washer and dryer unit for convenience

Plan #532-058D-0043
Price Code A

Total Living Area: 1,277 Sq. Ft.

Home has 3 bedrooms, 2 baths, 2-car garage and basement foundation.

Special features

- Vaulted ceilings in master bedroom, great room, kitchen and dining room
- Laundry closet is located near bedrooms for convenience
- Compact, yet efficient kitchen

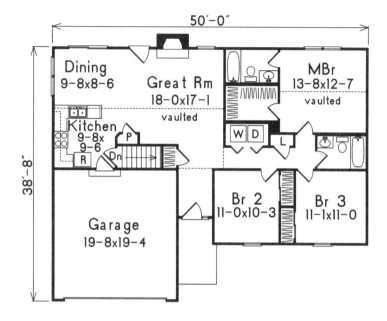

Plan #532-068D-0010
Price Code C

Total Living Area: 1,849 Sq. Ft.

Home has 3 bedrooms, 2 1/2 baths, 2-car side entry garage and slab foundation, drawings also include crawl space foundation.

Special features

■ Enormous laundry/mud room has many extras including storage area and half bath

■ Lavish master bath has corner jacuzzi tub, double sinks, separate shower and walk-in closet

■ Secondary bedrooms include walk-in closets

■ Kitchen has wrap-around eating counter and is positioned between formal dining area and breakfast room for convenience

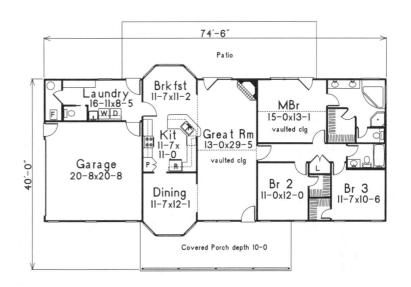

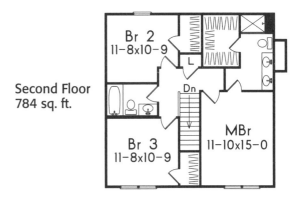

Second Floor
784 sq. ft.

Plan #532-058D-0038
Price Code B

Total Living Area: 1,680 Sq. Ft.

Home has 3 bedrooms, 2 1/2 baths, 2-car garage and basement foundation.

Special features

- Compact and efficient layout in an affordable package
- Second floor has three bedrooms all with oversized closets
- All bedrooms on second floor for privacy

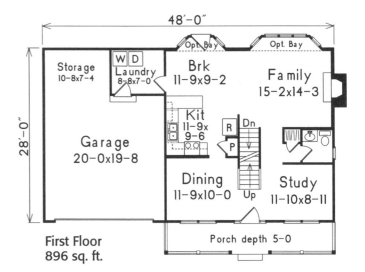

First Floor
896 sq. ft.

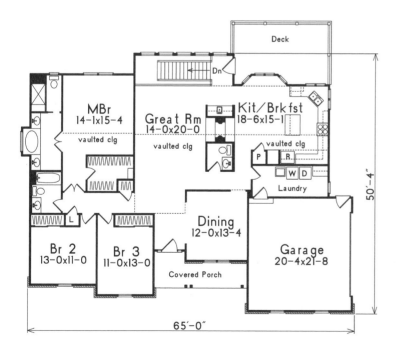

Plan #532-058D-0025
Price Code C
Total Living Area: 2,164 Sq. Ft.

Home has 3 bedrooms, 2 1/2 baths, 2-car side entry garage and basement foundation.

Special features
- Great design for entertaining with wet bar and see-through fireplace in great room
- Plenty of closet space
- Vaulted ceilings enlarge the master bedroom, great room and kitchen/breakfast area
- Great room features great view to the rear of the home

Second Floor
785 sq. ft.

Atrium below

Dn

Br 2
14-0x13-3

open to below

Balcony

Dn

Br 3
14-0x11-0

Br 4
12-3x12-9

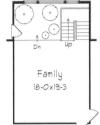

Family
18-0x19-3

Dn   Up

Lower Level
548 sq. ft.

54'-8"

51'-0"

Atrium below

Deck

Dn

Dining
10-2x13-3

Kit
11-0x
13-3

vaulted

Great Rm
18-0x19-10

vaulted

Bar

MBr
14-0x16-9

Foyer

Up

Porch

Garage
21-4x21-4

First Floor
1,473 sq. ft.

Plan #532-007D-0003
Price Code E

Total Living Area: 2,806 Sq. Ft.

Home has 4 bedrooms, 2 1/2 baths, 2-car garage and walk-out basement foundation.

Special features
- ■ Harmonious charm throughout
- ■ Sweeping balcony and vaulted ceiling soar above spacious great room and walk-in bar
- ■ Atrium with lower level family room is a unique touch, creating an open and airy feeling

Rear View

J.N. HANSEN S.D.G.

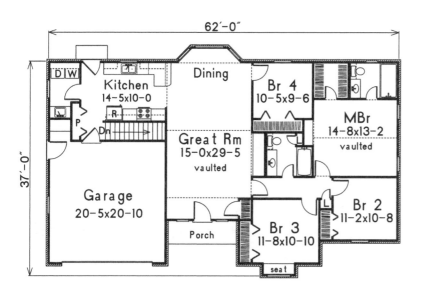

Plan #532-068D-0007
Price Code B
Total Living Area: 1,599 Sq. Ft.

Home has 4 bedrooms, 2 baths, 2-car garage and basement foundation, drawings also include crawl space and slab foundations.

Special features
- Efficiently designed kitchen with large pantry and easy access to laundry room
- Bedroom #3 has a charming window seat
- Master bedroom has a full bath and large walk-in closet

LOWE'S

Signature SERIES

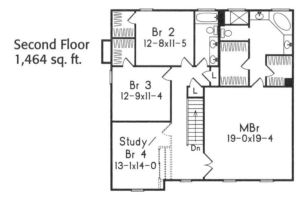

Second Floor
1,464 sq. ft.

Br 2
12-8x11-5

Br 3
12-9x11-4

Study/
Br 4
13-1x14-0

MBr
19-0x19-4

L

Dn

Plan #532-058D-0046
Price Code D

Total Living Area: 2,547 Sq. Ft.

Home has 3 bedrooms, 2 1/2 baths, 2-car garage and basement foundation.

Special features

- Second floor makes economical use of area above garage allowing for three bedrooms and a study/fourth bedroom
- First floor study is ideal for a home office
- Large pantry is located in efficient kitchen

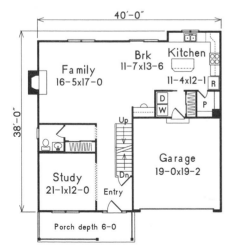

40'-0"

Family
16-5x17-0

Brk
11-7x13-6

Kitchen
11-4x12-1

38'-0"

D
W

R

P

Up

Study
21-1x12-0

Dn

Entry

Garage
19-0x19-2

Porch depth 6-0

First Floor
1,083 sq. ft.

Generous Closets In All The Bedrooms

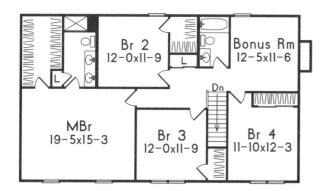

Br 2
12-0x11-9

Bonus Rm
12-5x11-6

Second Floor
1,344 sq. ft.

MBr
19-5x15-3

Br 3
12-0x11-9

Br 4
11-10x12-3

Dn

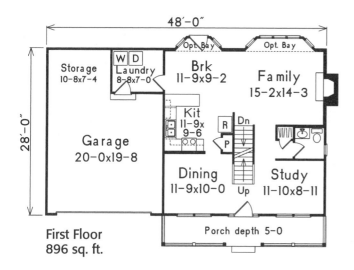

48'-0"

28'-0"

Storage
10-8x7-4

W D
Laundry
8-8x7-0

Brk
11-9x9-2

Family
15-2x14-3

Opt. Bay   Opt. Bay

Kit
11-9x
9-6

R
P

Dn

Garage
20-0x19-8

Dining
11-9x10-0

Up

Study
11-10x8-11

First Floor
896 sq. ft.

Porch depth 5-0

Plan #532-058D-0039
Price Code D
Total Living Area: 2,240 Sq. Ft.

Home has 4 bedrooms, 2 1/2 baths, 2-car garage and basement foundation.

Special features

- Floor plan makes good use of space above garage allowing for four bedrooms and a bonus room on the second floor
- Formal dining room easily accessible to kitchen
- Cozy family room with fireplace and sunny bay window
- Bonus room on the second floor is included in the square footage

Plan #532-007D-0067
Price Code B
Total Living Area: 1,761 Sq. Ft.

Home has 4 bedrooms, 2 baths, 2-car side entry garage and basement foundation.

Special features
- ■ Exterior window dressing, roof dormers and planter boxes provide visual warmth and charm
- ■ Great room boasts a vaulted ceiling, fireplace and opens to a pass-through kitchen
- ■ Master bedroom is vaulted with luxury bath and walk-in closet
- ■ Home features eight separate closets with an abundance of storage

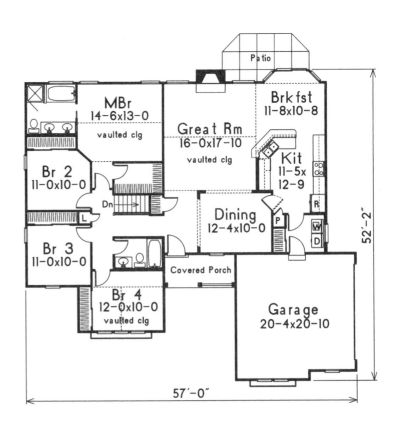

Plan #532-058D-0026
Price Code C

Total Living Area: 1,819 Sq. Ft.

Home has 3 bedrooms, 2 baths, 2-car side entry garage and basement foundation.

Special features

- Master bedroom features access to the outdoors, large walk-in closet and private bath
- 9' ceilings throughout
- Formal foyer with coat closet opens into vaulted great room with fireplace and formal dining room
- Kitchen and breakfast room create a cozy and casual area

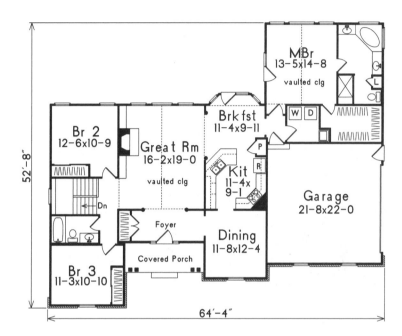

Inviting Gabled Entry

Plan #532-068D-0009
Price Code C

Total Living Area: 2,128 Sq. Ft.

Home has 4 bedrooms, 2 baths, 2-car garage and slab foundation, drawings also include crawl space foundation.

Special features

- Versatile kitchen has plenty of space for entertaining with large dining area and counter seating
- Luxurious master bedroom has double-door entry and private bath with jacuzzi tub, double sinks and large walk-in closet
- Secondary bedrooms include spacious walk-in closets
- Coat closet in front entry is a nice added feature

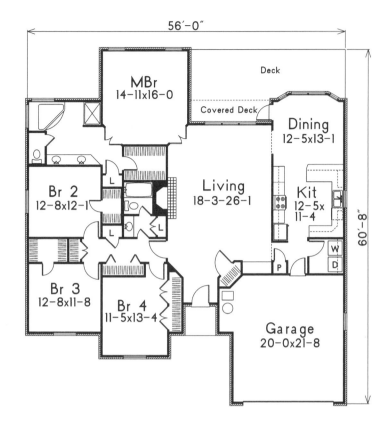

Second Floor
511 sq. ft.

Plan #532-034D-0014
Price Code B
Total Living Area: 1,792 Sq. Ft.

Home has 3 bedrooms, 2 1/2 baths,
2-car garage and basement foundation.

Special features
- ■ Traditional styling makes this a
  popular design
- ■ First floor master bedroom maintains privacy
- ■ Dining area has sliding glass doors
  leading to the outdoors
- ■ Formal dining and living rooms
  combine for added gathering space

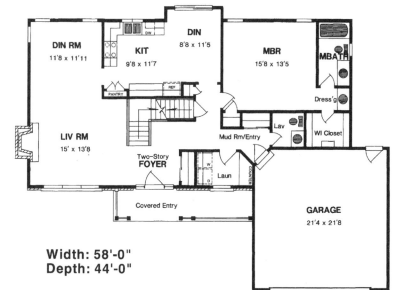

First Floor
1,281 sq. ft.

Width: 58'-0"
Depth: 44'-0"

Plan #532-056D-0009
Price Code B
Total Living Area: 1,606 Sq. Ft.

Home has 3 bedrooms, 2 baths, 2-car garage and slab foundation.

Special features
- Kitchen has a snack bar which overlooks the dining area for convenience
- Master bedroom has lots of windows with a private bath and large walk-in closet
- Cathedral vault in great room adds spaciousness

Width: 50'-0"
Depth: 42'-0"

Quaint Country Home

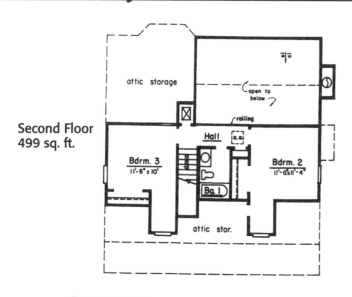

Second Floor
499 sq. ft.

Plan #532-024D-0010
Price Code B

Total Living Area: 1,737 Sq. Ft.

Home has 3 bedrooms, 2 1/2 baths and slab or crawl space foundation, please specify when ordering.

Special features

- U-shaped kitchen, sunny bayed breakfast room and living area become one large gathering area

- Living area has a sloped ceiling and balcony overlook from the second floor

- Second floor includes lots of storage area

Width: 36'-0"
Depth: 49'-0"

First Floor
1,238 sq. ft.

Plan #532-008D-0054
Price Code B

Total Living Area: 1,574 Sq. Ft.

Home has 3 bedrooms, 2 baths, 2-car garage and basement foundation, drawings also include crawl space foundation.

Special features

- Foyer enters into open great room with corner fireplace and rear dining room with adjoining kitchen
- Two secondary bedrooms share a full bath
- Master bedroom has a spacious private bath
- Garage accesses home through mud room/laundry

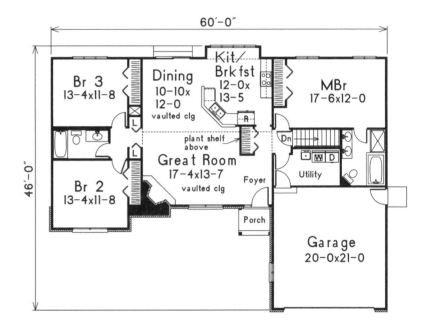

Plan #532-035D-0021
Price Code C

Total Living Area: 1,978 Sq. Ft.

Home has 3 bedrooms, 2 1/2 baths, 2-car garage and walk-out basement, slab or crawl space foundation, please specify when ordering.

Special features
- ■ Elegant arched openings through-out interior
- ■ Vaulted living room off foyer
- ■ Master suite features a cheerful sitting room and a private bath

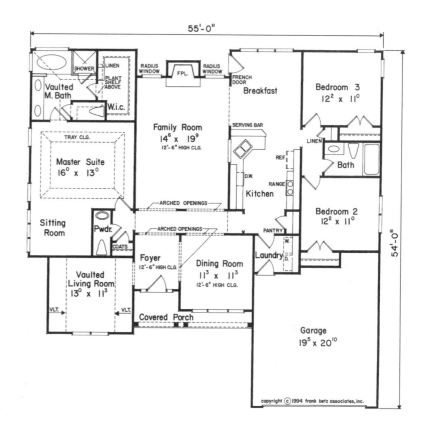

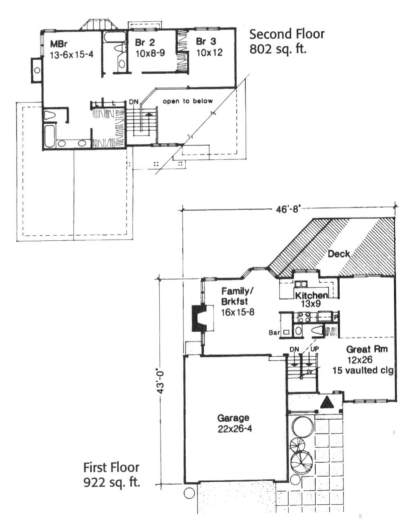

Second Floor
802 sq. ft.

MBr
13-6x15-4

Br 2
10x8-9

Br 3
10x12

DN

open to below

Plan #532-072D-0001
Price Code B

Total Living Area: 1,724 Sq. Ft.

Home has 3 bedrooms, 2 1/2 baths, 2-car garage and basement foundation.

Special features

- Beautiful palladian windows enliven the two-story entry
- Sliding glass doors in the formal dining room connect to the large backyard deck
- Second floor master bedroom boasts corner windows, large walk-in closet and a split bath

---

46'-8"

Deck

Family/
Brkfst
16x15-8

Kitchen
13x9

Bar

DN   UP

Great Rm
12x26
15 vaulted clg

43'-0"

Garage
22x26-4

First Floor
922 sq. ft.

Plan #532-026D-0155
Price Code B

Total Living Area: 1,691 Sq. Ft.

Home has 3 bedrooms, 2 baths, 2-car garage and basement foundation.

Special features

- Bay windowed breakfast room allows for plenty of sunlight
- Large inviting covered porch in the front of the home
- Great room fireplace is surrounded by windows

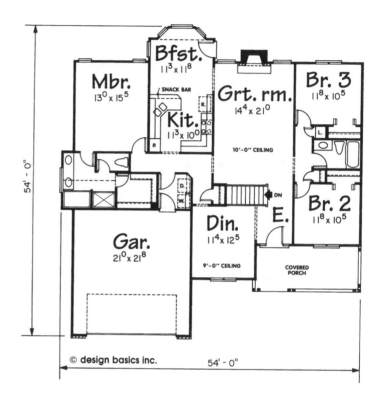

Plan #532-055D-0017
Price Code B
Total Living Area: 1,525 Sq. Ft.

Home has 3 bedrooms, 2 baths, 2-car garage and basement, walk-out basement, crawl space or slab foundation, please specify when ordering.

Special features
- Corner fireplace is highlighted in the great room
- Unique glass block window over whirlpool tub in master bath brightens interior
- Open bar overlooks both the kitchen and great room
- Breakfast room leads to an outdoor grilling and covered porch

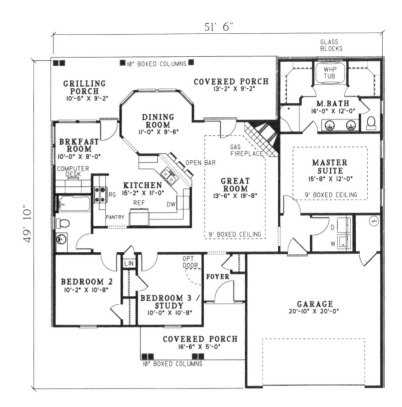

Plan #532-008D-0001
Price Code C

Total Living Area: 2,137 Sq. Ft.

Home has 4 bedrooms, 2 1/2 baths, 2-car garage and basement foundation.

Special features

- Foyer leads to a majestic-sized living room with masonry fireplace

- Family room has a beamed ceiling and adjoins a very spacious kitchen

- Oversized laundry room features a full closet and convenient service sink

- Gallery-sized second floor hall leads to a roomy compartmented hall bath with double-bowl vanity

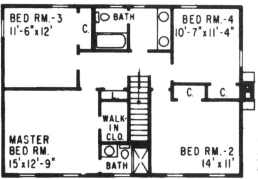

Second Floor
988 sq. ft.

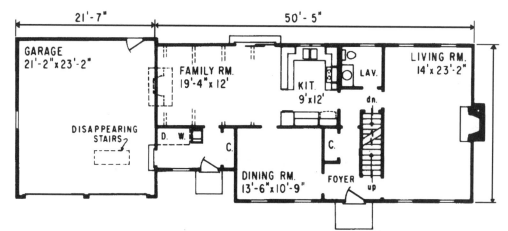

First Floor
1,149 sq. ft.

Plan #532-026D-0112
Price Code C

Total Living Area: 1,911 Sq. Ft.

Home has 3 bedrooms, 2 baths, 2-car garage and basement foundation.

Special features

■ Large entry opens into a beautiful great room with an angled see-through fireplace

■ Terrific design includes kitchen and breakfast area with adjacent sunny bayed hearth room

■ Private master bedroom with bath features skylight and walk-in closet

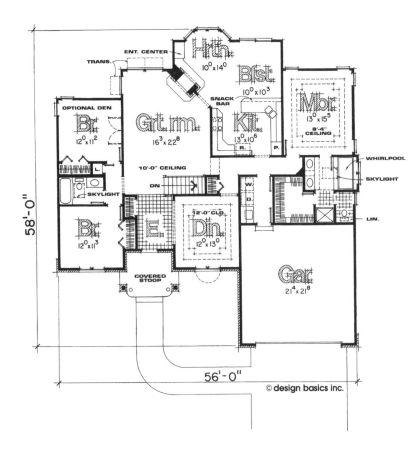

© design basics inc.

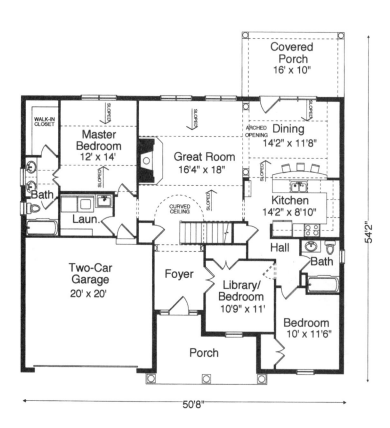

Plan #532-065D-0032
Price Code B

Total Living Area: 1,544 Sq. Ft.

Home has 3 bedrooms, 2 baths, 2-car garage and basement foundation.

Special features

- ■ A curved countertop with seating creates a delightful bar for quick meals

- ■ A double-door entrance off the foyer enables one bedroom to function as a library offering flexibility

- ■ Arched openings and sloped ceilings are nice additions to the design

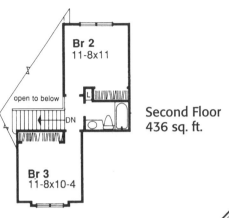

Br 2
11-8x11

open to below

DN

Second Floor
436 sq. ft.

Br 3
11-8x10-4

Plan #532-072D-0004
Price Code C

Total Living Area: 1,926 Sq. Ft.

Home has 3 bedrooms, 3 baths, 2-car garage and basement foundation.

Special features

- A breathtaking wall of windows brightens the great room
- A double-door entry leads to the master suite which features a large bath and walk-in closet
- An island cooktop in the kitchen makes mealtime a breeze

55'-8"

Deck

Great Rm
14x18-6
16 vaulted clg

Kit
11x12

Glass Above

Brkfst
11x10
12 vaulted clg

Pantry   Desk

UP   DN

D   W

45'-0"

Mas. Suite
13x16
14 vaulted clg

Dining
11-6x12-3

Garage
20x20

First Floor
1,490 sq. ft.

Plan #532-052D-0005
Price Code A

Total Living Area: 1,268 Sq. Ft.

Home has 3 bedrooms, 2 baths, 2-car drive under garage and basement foundation.

Special features

- Raised gable porch is a focal point creating a dramatic look
- 10' ceilings throughout living and dining areas
- Open kitchen is well designed
- Master bedroom offers a tray ceiling and private bath with both a garden tub and a 4' shower

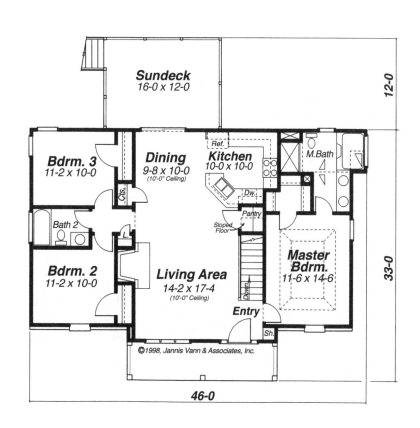

Plan #532-039D-0018
Price Code C

Total Living Area: 2,008 Sq. Ft.

Home has 4 bedrooms, 2 1/2 baths, 2-car garage and basement foundation.

Special features

- Family room has character with 15' ceiling, fireplace and columns separating it from breakfast area and kitchen
- Inviting two-story foyer with plant shelves
- Private master suite enjoys porch views

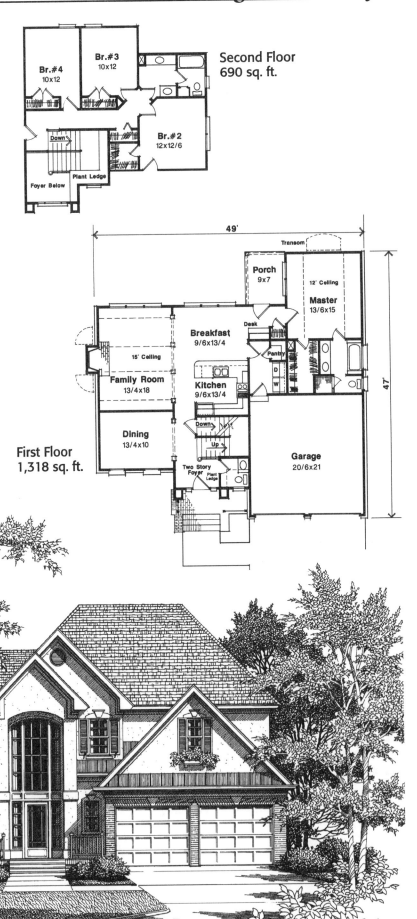

Second Floor
690 sq. ft.

Br.#4
10x12

Br.#3
10x12

Br.#2
12x12/6

Down

Plant Ledge

Foyer Below

49'

47'

Transom

Porch
9x7

12' Ceiling

Master
13/6x15

Breakfast
9/6x13/4

Desk

Pantry

Family Room
13/4x18

15' Ceiling

Kitchen
9/6x13/4

D
W

First Floor
1,318 sq. ft.

Dining
13/4x10

Down

Up

Two Story
Foyer

Plant
Ledge

Garage
20/6x21

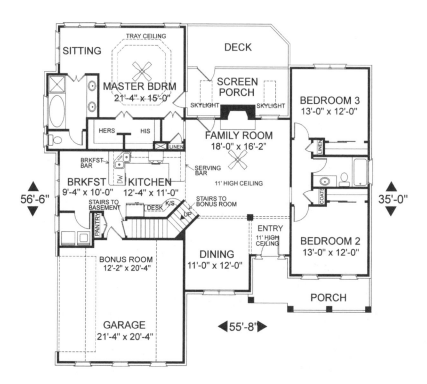

Plan #532-013D-0015
Price Code B
Total Living Area: 1,787 Sq. Ft.

Home has 3 bedrooms, 2 baths, 2-car side entry garage and basement, crawl space or slab foundation, please specify when ordering.

Special features
- Skylights brighten screen porch which connects to the family room and deck outdoors
- Master bedroom features a comfortable sitting area, large private bath and direct access to screen porch
- Kitchen has a serving bar which extends dining into the family room

Plan #532-019D-0009
Price Code C

Total Living Area: 1,862 Sq. Ft.

Home has 3 bedrooms, 2 baths, 2-car garage and crawl space foundation, drawings also include slab foundation.

Special features

- Comfortable traditional has all the amenities of a larger plan in a compact layout

- Angled eating bar separates kitchen and great room while leaving these areas open to one another for entertaining

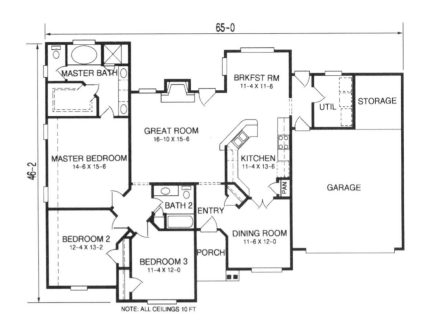

NOTE: ALL CEILINGS 10 FT

Second Floor
441 sq. ft.

BED RM. 2
11'-0" X 10'-8"

BED RM. 3
9'-3" X 11'-0"

ATTIC STORAGE

4" WALL

5' WALL

48' 0"

43' 0"

GLASS BLOCKS

WHP TUB
M. BATH
SEAT SHWR
KNEE SPACE LIN
STRG. 6'-0" X 4'-0"
WH

MASTER SUITE
15'-0" X 13'-3"

MEDIA CENTER

GREAT RM.
16'-2" X 18'-0"

LAU.
7'-2" X 6'-0"

GARAGE
19'-0" X 20'-0"

REF.
RG.
KITCHEN
9'-10" X 11'-0"
DW

PAN

FOYER
10' CLNG

8" COLUMNS

BRKFAST RM.
9'-10" X 8'-0"

DINING RM.
10' CLNG
11'-6" X 12'-6"

PRCH

First Floor
1,356 sq. ft.

Plan #532-055D-0044
Price Code B
Total Living Area: 1,797 Sq. Ft.

Home has 3 bedrooms, 2 1/2 baths, 2-car garage and walk-out basement, basement, crawl space or slab foundation, please specify when ordering.

Special features
- ◼ Great room has outdoor access, media center and a fireplace
- ◼ Attractive dormers add character to second floor bedrooms
- ◼ Efficiently designed kitchen
- ◼ Formal dining area is separated from other areas for entertaining

Plan #532-072D-0002
Price Code A

Total Living Area: 1,551 Sq. Ft.

Home has 3 bedrooms, 3 baths, 2-car garage and basement foundation.

Special features

- Vaulted dining room has a view onto the patio
- Master suite is vaulted with a private bath and walk-in closet
- An arched entry leads to the vaulted living room featuring tall windows and a fireplace

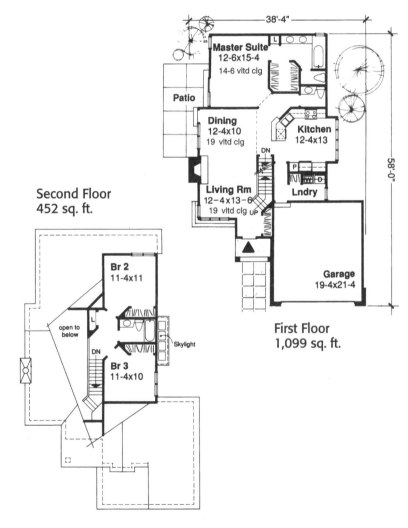

Second Floor
452 sq. ft.

First Floor
1,099 sq. ft.

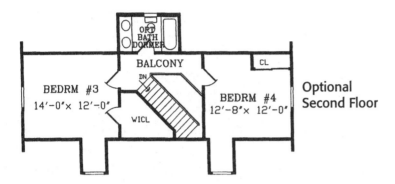

Optional
Second Floor

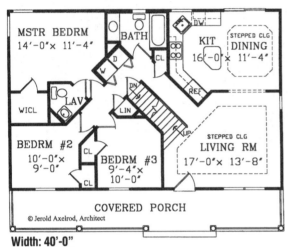

First Floor
1,040 sq. ft.

Width: 40'-0"
Depth: 26'-0"

Plan #532-016D-0055
Price Code B
Total Living Area: 1,040 Sq. Ft.

Home has 3 bedrooms, 1 1/2 baths and crawl space, slab or basement foundation, please specify when ordering.

Special features

■ An island in the kitchen greatly simplifies your food preparation efforts

■ A wide archway joins the formal living room to the dramatic angled kitchen and dining room

■ Optional second floor has an additional 597 square feet of living area

■ Optional first floor design has 2 bedrooms including a large master bedroom that enjoys a private luxury bath

Plan #532-035D-0011
Price Code C
Total Living Area: 1,945 Sq. Ft.

Home has 4 bedrooms, 2 baths, 2-car side entry garage and walk-out basement, crawl space or slab foundation, please specify when ordering.

Special features
- Master suite is separate from other bedrooms for privacy
- Vaulted breakfast room is directly off great room
- Kitchen includes a built-in desk area
- Elegant dining room has an arched window

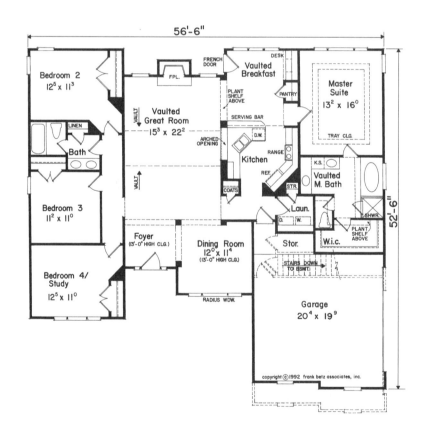

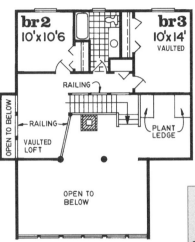

First Floor
1,157 sq. ft.

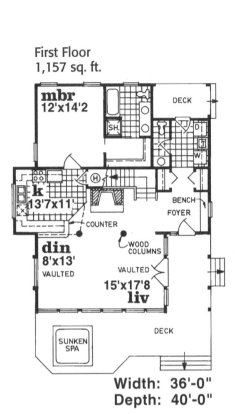

Second Floor
638 sq. ft.

Width: 36'-0"
Depth: 40'-0"

Plan #532-062D-0052
Price Code B

Total Living Area: 1,795 Sq. Ft.

Home has 3 bedrooms, 2 1/2 baths and basement or crawl space foundation, please specify when ordering.

Special features
- Window wall in living and dining areas brings the outdoors in
- Master bedroom has a full bath and walk-in closet
- Vaulted loft on second floor is a unique feature

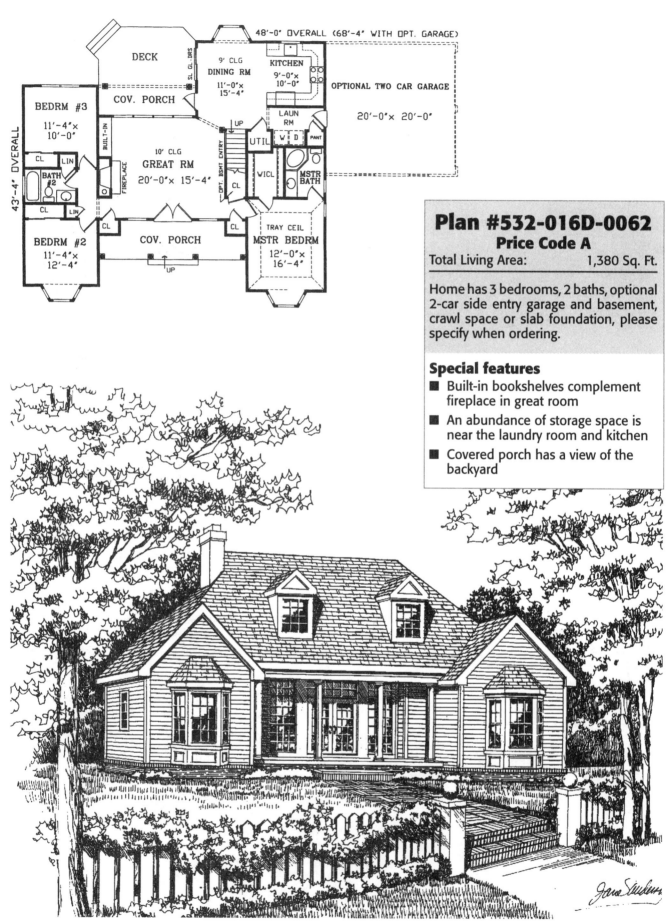

48'-0" OVERALL (68'-4" WITH OPT. GARAGE)

DECK

9' CLG
DINING RM
11'-0" x
15'-4"

KITCHEN
9'-0" x
10'-0"

SL. GL. DRS.

COV. PORCH

OPTIONAL TWO CAR GARAGE
20'-0" x 20'-0"

BEDRM #3
11'-4" x
10'-0"

BUILT-IN

LAUN
RM

UP

43'-4" OVERALL

10' CLG
GREAT RM
20'-0" x 15'-4"

FIREPLACE

OPT. BSMT. ENTRY

UTIL

W D

PANT

CL

BATH
#2

WICL

MSTR
BATH

CL

CL

LIN

CL

LIN

BEDRM #2
11'-4" x
12'-4"

CL

COV. PORCH

UP

CL

TRAY CEIL
MSTR BEDRM
12'-0" x
16'-4"

Plan #532-016D-0062
Price Code A

Total Living Area: 1,380 Sq. Ft.

Home has 3 bedrooms, 2 baths, optional 2-car side entry garage and basement, crawl space or slab foundation, please specify when ordering.

Special features

■ Built-in bookshelves complement fireplace in great room

■ An abundance of storage space is near the laundry room and kitchen

■ Covered porch has a view of the backyard

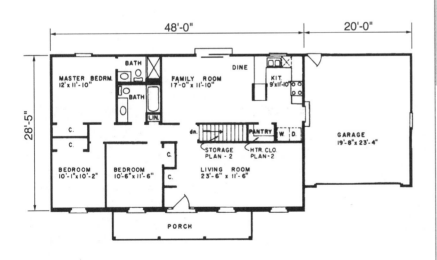

Plan #532-008D-0122
Price Code A
Total Living Area: 1,364 Sq. Ft.

Home has 3 bedrooms, 2 baths, 2-car garage and basement foundation, drawings also include crawl space and slab foundations.

Special features
- A large porch and entry door with sidelights lead into a generous living room
- Well-planned U-shaped kitchen features a laundry closet, built-in pantry and open peninsula
- Master bedroom has its own bath with 4' shower
- Convenient to the kitchen is an oversized two-car garage with service door to rear

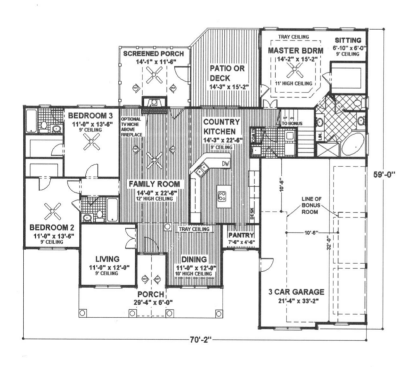

Plan #532-013D-0025
Price Code C

Total Living Area: 2,097 SQ. Ft.

Home has 3 bedrooms, 3 baths, 3-car side entry garage and crawl space or slab foundation, please specify when ordering.

Special features

- Angled kitchen, family room and eating area adds interest to this home

- Family room includes a TV niche making this a cozy place to relax

- Sumptuous master bedroom includes sitting area, double walk-in closet and a full bath with double vanities

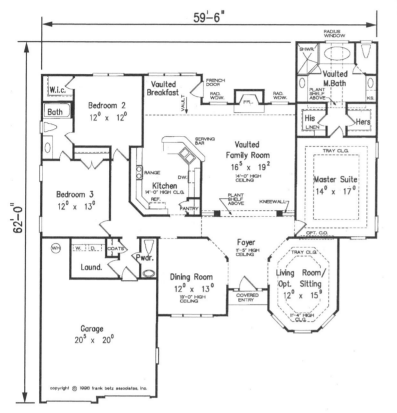

59'-6"

62'-0"

W.i.c.

Bath

Bedroom 2
12⁰ x 12⁰

Vaulted
Breakfast

FRENCH
DOOR

RAD.
WDW.

FPL.

RAD.
WDW.

RADIUS
WINDOW

SHWR

Vaulted
M.Bath

PLANT
SHELF
ABOVE

W.S.

His

LINEN

Hers

Bedroom 3
12⁰ x 13⁰

RANGE

SERVING
BAR

Kitchen
14'-0" HIGH CLG.

DW.

REF.

PANTRY

PLANT
SHELF
ABOVE

Vaulted
Family Room
16⁵ x 19²
14'-0" HIGH
CEILING

KNEEWALL

TRAY CLG.

Master Suite
14⁰ x 17⁰

OPT. C.O.

WH

W. D. COATS

Laund.

Pwdr.

Dining Room
12⁰ x 13⁰
13'-0" HIGH
CEILING

Foyer
11'-5" HIGH
CEILING

COVERED
ENTRY

TRAY CLG.

Living Room/
Opt. Sitting
12⁰ x 15⁹
11'-4" HIGH
CLG.

Garage
20⁵ x 20⁰

copyright © 1996 frank betz associates, inc.

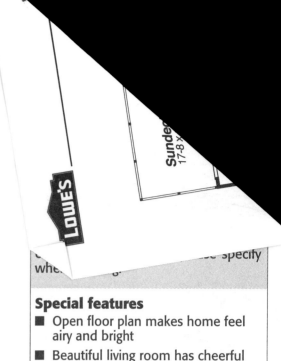

LOWE'S

...be specify
whe...

Special features
- Open floor plan makes home feel airy and bright
- Beautiful living room has cheerful bay window
- Master suite has two walk-in closets
- Family room, kitchen and breakfast area combine for added space

Deck
12-0

Dining
10-2 x 11-10

Kit.
10-0 x 11-6

Dw.

Bkfst Bar

Ref.

Bdrm.3
11-6 x 10-6

Bdrm.2
11-6 x 12-8

W. D. Lin.

Living Area
20-2 x 13-6
Flat Ceil. 11-6 High

Cts.

Dn.

Tray Ceil.

Master Bdrm.
12-6 x 13-6

Entry

M.Bath
Ks.

©1998, Jannis Vann & Associates, Inc.

12-0

32-0

48-0

Plan #532-052D-0013
Price Code A
Total Living Area: 1,379 Sq. Ft.

Home has 3 bedrooms, 2 baths, 2-car drive under garage and basement foundation.

Special features
- Living area has spacious feel with 11'-6" ceiling
- Kitchen has eat-in breakfast bar open to dining area
- Laundry is located near the bedrooms
- Large cased opening with columns opens to the living and dining areas

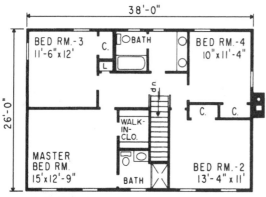

Second Floor
988 sq. ft.

38'-0"

26'-0"

BED RM.-3
11'-6"x12'

BATH
C.
L

BED RM.-4
10"x11'-4"

UP

WALK-
IN-
CLO.

C. C.

MASTER
BED RM.
15'x12'-9"

BATH

BED RM.-2
13'-4" x 11'

Plan #532-008D-0008
Price Code C
Total Living Area: 2,137 Sq. Ft.

Home has 4 bedrooms, 2 1/2 baths,
2-car garage and partial basement/
crawl space foundation.

Special features

- ■ Spacious porch for plants, chairs
  and family gatherings
- ■ Huge living room includes front and
  rear views
- ■ U-shaped kitchen features abundant
  storage
- ■ Laundry room with large closet has
  its own porch

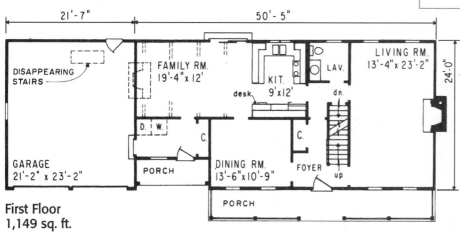

21'-7"

50'-5"

24'-0"

DISAPPEARING
STAIRS

FAMILY RM.
19'-4"x12'

KIT.
9'x12'

LAV.

LIVING RM.
13'-4"x 23'-2"

desk

dn.

D. W.

C.

C.

GARAGE
21'-2" x 23'-2"

PORCH

DINING RM.
13'-6"x10'-9"

FOYER

up

PORCH

First Floor
1,149 sq. ft.

Plan #532-008D-0089
Price Code C

Total Living Area: 1,907 Sq. Ft.

Home has 3 bedrooms, 2 baths, 2-car garage and partial basement/crawl space foundation.

Special features

- Entry foyer opens to kitchen and breakfast area on the right and a large activity area on the left

- Activity area amenities include a fireplace and sun room

- Formal dining area with bay windows and sliding glass doors located at rear of kitchen

- Master bedroom has double walk-in closets and a double-vanity sink

- Two additional bedrooms share one full bath

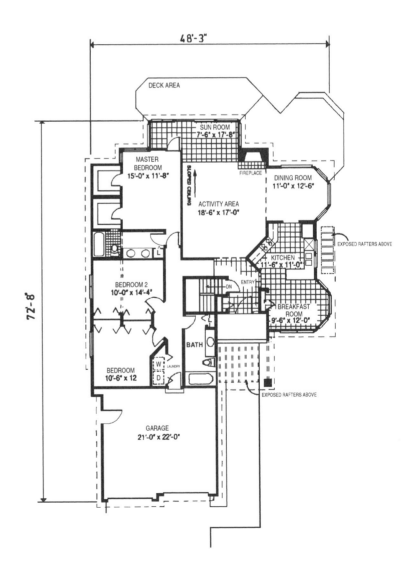

Second Floor
579 sq. ft.

STORAGE

BEDROOM 3
15X12

OPEN TO BELOW

DN

BEDROOM 2
15X12

Plan #532-013D-0011
Price Code B

Total Living Area: 1,643 Sq. Ft.

Home has 3 bedrooms, 2 1/2 baths, 2-car drive under garage and basement or crawl space foundation, please specify when ordering.

Special features

■ First floor master bedroom has a private bath, walk-in closet and easy access to the laundry closet

■ Comfortable family room features a vaulted ceiling and a cozy fireplace

■ Two bedrooms on the second floor share a bath

DECK

DINING
12x12

KITCHEN
10x12

SKYLIGHT

VAULT

COATS

D

W

DN

VAULT

UP

MASTER BEDRM
15x13

FAMILY ROOM
18x15

34

First Floor
1,064 sq. ft.

38

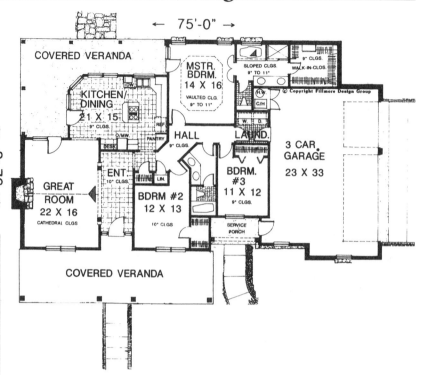

Plan #532-036D-0048
Price Code C

Total Living Area: 1,830 Sq. Ft.

Home has 3 bedrooms, 2 baths, 3-car side entry garage and basement, crawl space or slab foundation, please specify when ordering.

Special features

- ■ Inviting covered verandas in the front and rear of the home
- ■ Great room has a fireplace and cathedral ceiling
- ■ Handy service porch allows easy access
- ■ Master bedroom has a vaulted ceiling and private bath

50—0 WIDE X 42—0 DEEP
(INCLUDING COVERED PORCH)

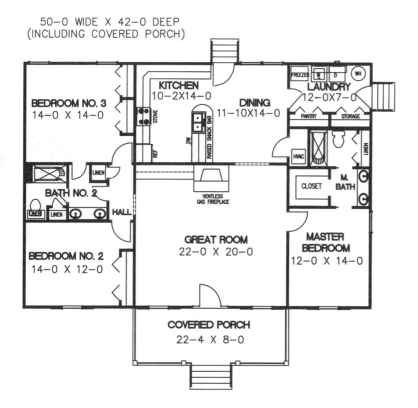

Plan #532-028D-0006
Price Code B
Total Living Area: 1,700 Sq. Ft.

Home has 3 bedrooms, 2 baths and crawl space foundation.

Special features
- Oversized laundry room has large pantry and storage area as well as access to the outdoors
- Master bedroom is separated from other bedrooms for privacy
- Raised snack bar in kitchen allows extra seating for dining

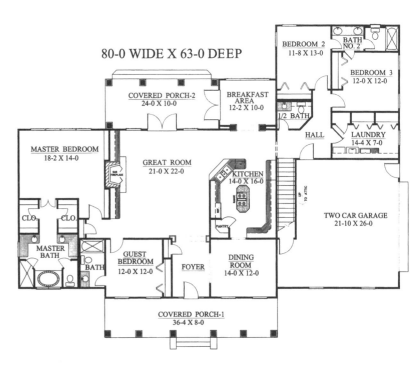

Plan #532-028D-0017
Price Code E
Total Living Area: 2,669 Sq. Ft.

Home has 4 bedrooms, 3 1/2 baths, 2-car side entry garage and basement, crawl space or slab foundation, please specify when ordering.

Special features
■ Nice-sized corner pantry in kitchen

■ Guest bedroom, located off the great room, has a full bath and would make an excellent office

■ Master bath has double walk-in closets, whirlpool tub and a large shower

80-0 WIDE X 63-0 DEEP

BEDROOM 2
11-8 X 13-0

BATH NO. 2

BEDROOM 3
12-0 X 12-0

COVERED PORCH-2
24-0 X 10-0

BREAKFAST AREA
12-2 X 10-0

1/2 BATH

HALL

LAUNDRY
14-4 X 7-0

MASTER BEDROOM
18-2 X 14-0

GREAT ROOM
21-0 X 22-0

KITCHEN
14-0 X 16-0

GAS FIREPLACE

UP TO ATTIC

TWO CAR GARAGE
21-10 X 26-0

CLO.

CLO.

PANTRY

MASTER BATH

BATH

GUEST BEDROOM
12-0 X 12-0

FOYER

DINING ROOM
14-0 X 12-0

COVERED PORCH-1
36-4 X 8-0

Cozy Corner Fireplace

Plan #532-011D-0022
Price Code D
Total Living Area: 1,994 Sq. Ft.

Home has 3 bedrooms, 2 1/2 baths, 2-car garage and crawl space foundation.

Special features

- Breakfast nook overlooks the kitchen and great room creating an airy feeling
- A double-door entry off the family room leads to a cozy den ideal as a home office
- Master suite has a walk-in closet and private bath

Second Floor
882 sq. ft.

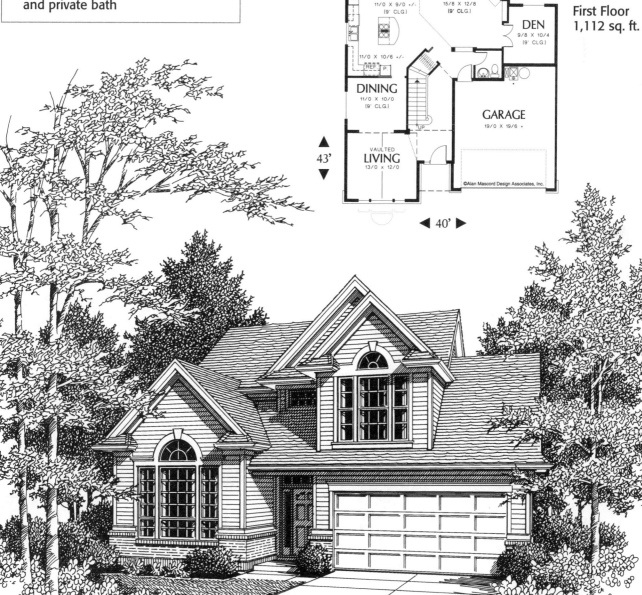

First Floor
1,112 sq. ft.

43'

40'

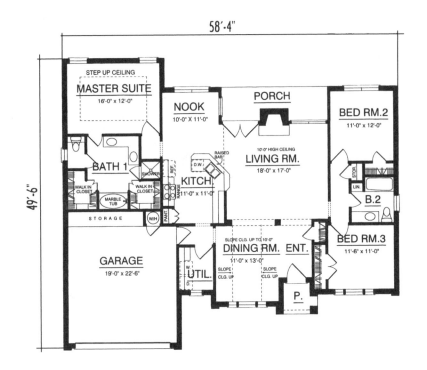

Plan #532-030D-0004
Price Code B
Total Living Area: 1,791 Sq. Ft.

Home has 3 bedrooms, 2 baths, 2-car garage and slab or crawl space foundation, please specify when ordering.

Special features
- Dining area has a 10' high sloped ceiling
- Kitchen opens to the large living room with fireplace and has access to a covered porch
- Master suite features a private bath, double walk-in closets and whirlpool tub

COPYRIGHT LARRY E. BELK

WIDTH 48–10

OPTIONAL BAY WINDOW

FP

LIN

MASTER BATH

DINING
9-8 X 9-6
10 FT CLG

LIVING ROOM
16-0 X 17-6
10 FT CLG

BEDRM 3
10-0 X 10-0

SLOPE

MASTER BEDRM
11-0 X 14-0
10 FT CLG

10 FT CLG
KITCHEN
13-4 X 9-6

ARCH

FOYER

ARCH

BATH 2

LIN

BEDRM 2
10-0 X 12-0

DEPTH 52-6

STORAGE

PORCH

COPYRIGHT LARRY E. BELK

GARAGE

Plan #532-019D-0002
Price Code A

Total Living Area: 1,282 Sq. Ft.

Home has 3 bedrooms, 2 baths, 2-car garage and crawl space foundation, drawings also include slab foundation.

Special features

- Angled entry creates the illusion of space making the home appear larger
- Dining room serves both formal and informal occasions
- Master bedroom has a walk-in closet and private bath with whirlpool/shower combination

© Michael E. Nelson
NELSON DESIGN GROUP, LLC

Plan #532-055D-0030
Price Code C

Total Living Area: 2,107 Sq. Ft.

Home has 4 bedrooms, 2 1/2 baths, 2-car garage and crawl space, basement, walk-out basement or slab foundation, please specify when ordering.

Special features

- Master bedroom is separate from other bedrooms for privacy

- Spacious breakfast room and kitchen include center island with eating space

- Centralized great room has fireplace and easy access to any area in the home

Comfortable Family Living

Width: 46'-0"
Depth: 49'-2"

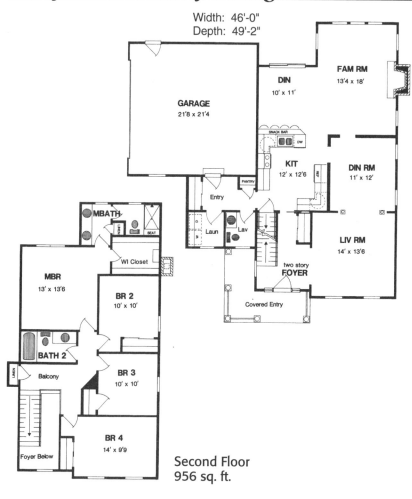

First Floor
1,141 sq. ft.

GARAGE
21'8 x 21'4

DIN
10' x 11'

FAM RM
13'4 x 18'

SNACK BAR   DW

KIT
12' x 12'6

PANTRY

Entry

DIN RM
11' x 12'

Laun   Lav

two story
FOYER

LIV RM
14' x 13'6

Covered Entry

MBATH

SEAT

WI Closet

MBR
13' x 13'6

BR 2
10' x 10'

BATH 2

Balcony

LINEN

BR 3
10' x 10'

BR 4
14' x 9'9

Foyer Below

Second Floor
956 sq. ft.

Plan #532-034D-0022
Price Code C

Total Living Area: 2,097 Sq. Ft.

Home has 4 bedrooms, 2 1/2 baths, 2-car side entry garage and basement foundation.

Special features

- Formal living room connects with the dining room, perfect for entertaining
- Elegant two-story foyer
- Spacious entry off the garage is near a bath and laundry area
- Family room has a cozy fireplace

MAXON

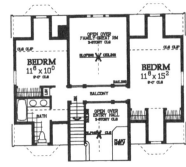

Second Floor
600 sq. ft.

Plan #532-049D-0006
Price Code B

Total Living Area: 1,771 Sq. Ft.

Home has 3 bedrooms, 2 1/2 baths, optional detached 2-car garage and basement foundation.

Special features

- Efficient country kitchen shares space with a bayed eating area
- Two-story family/great room is warmed by a fireplace in winter and open to outdoor country comfort in the summer with double French doors
- First floor master suite offers a bay window and access to the porch through French doors

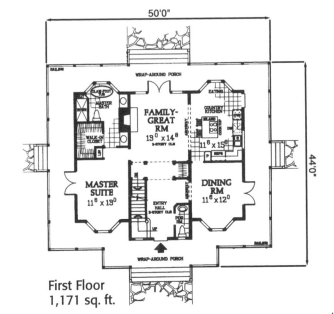

First Floor
1,171 sq. ft.

Plan #532-035D-0036
Price Code C
Total Living Area: 2,193 Sq. Ft.

Home has 3 bedrooms, 3 baths, 2-car side entry garage and walk-out basement, crawl space or slab foundation, please specify when ordering.

Special features
- Master suite includes a sitting room
- Dining room has decorative columns and overlooks family room
- Kitchen has lots of storage
- Optional bonus room with bath on second floor has an additional 400 square feet of living area

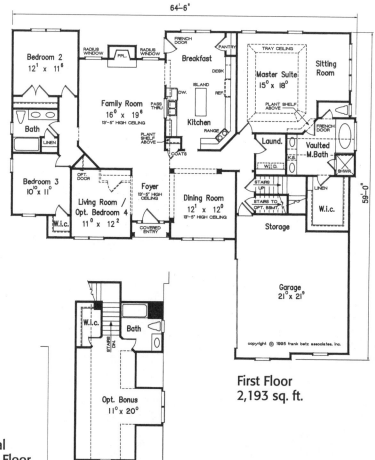

First Floor
2,193 sq. ft.

Optional
Second Floor

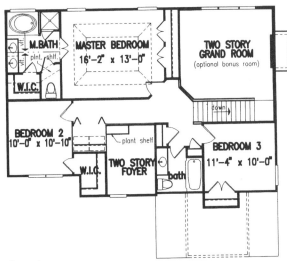

Second Floor
843 sq. ft.

Plan #532-056D-0022
Price Code C
Total Living Area: 1,817 Sq. Ft.

Home has 3 bedrooms, 2 1/2 baths, 2-car garage and basement or slab foundation, please specify when ordering.

Special features

- Two-story foyer is accented with a plant shelf

- Living and dining rooms are separated by distinctive columns

- Laundry area is located on the second floor near the bedrooms

- Two-story grand room has a fireplace and second floor balcony

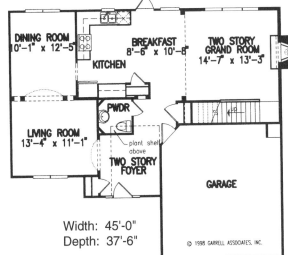

First Floor
974 sq. ft.

Width: 45'-0"
Depth: 37'-6"

© 1998 GARRELL ASSOCIATES, INC.

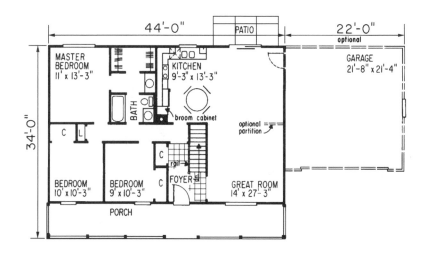

Plan #532-008D-0012
Price Code A

Total Living Area: 1,232 Sq. Ft.

Home has 3 bedrooms, 1 bath, optional 2-car garage and basement foundation, drawings also include crawl space and slab foundations.

Special features

- Ideal porch for quiet quality evenings
- Great room opens to dining room for those large dinner gatherings
- Functional L-shaped kitchen includes broom cabinet
- Master bedroom contains a large walk-in closet and compartmented bath

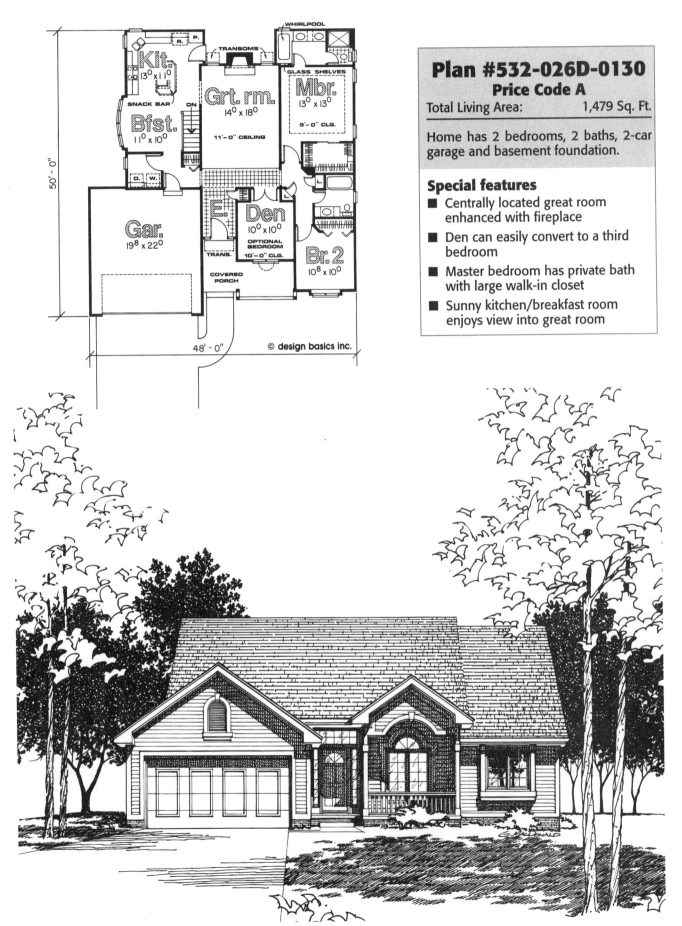

Plan #532-026D-0130
Price Code A
Total Living Area: 1,479 SQ. Ft.

Home has 2 bedrooms, 2 baths, 2-car garage and basement foundation.

Special features
- Centrally located great room enhanced with fireplace
- Den can easily convert to a third bedroom
- Master bedroom has private bath with large walk-in closet
- Sunny kitchen/breakfast room enjoys view into great room

© design basics inc.

Second Floor
576 sq. ft.

First Floor
1,093 sq. ft.

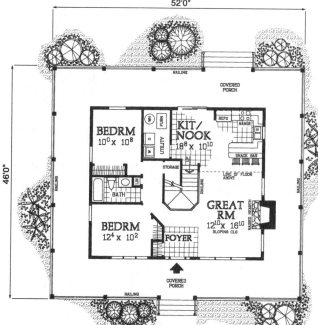

Plan #532-049D-0010
Price Code B

Total Living Area: 1,669 Sq. Ft.

Home has 3 bedrooms, 2 baths and crawl space foundation.

Special features

- Windows add exciting visual elements to the exterior as well as plenty of natural light to the interior

- Two-story great room has a raised hearth

- Second floor loft/study would easily make a terrific home office

DECK

MASTER BED.
14'-0" x 12'-4"

KIT
11'-0" x 9'-0"

DINING
10'-0" x 12'-4"
12'-0" clg

DN

CLERESTORY
ABOVE

LIVING
13'-0" x 15'-8"
17'-0" vaulted clg

GARAGE
18'-4" x 18'-4"

UP

37'-8"

38'-8"

First Floor
894 sq. ft.

Second Floor
423 sq. ft.

LOFT/
BDRM 3
12'-0" x 12'-4"

BDRM 2
9'-8" x 12'-8"

DN

OPEN TO BELOW

Plan #532-072D-0003
Price Code A

Total Living Area: 1,317 Sq. Ft.

Home has 3 bedrooms, 2 baths, 2-car garage and basement foundation.

Special features

■ A large window topped by a clere-story window gives the living room a bright, airy feel

■ A three-way fireplace defines the space between the living and dining rooms

■ An efficient kitchen neatly serves the dining room

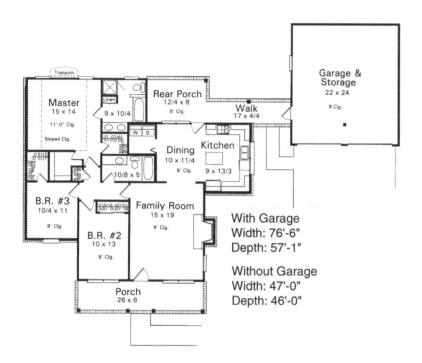

Garage & Storage
22 x 24
8' Clg.

Master
15 x 14
11'-0" Clg.
Sloped Clg.

Transom

Linen

Rear Porch
12/4 x 8
8' Clg.

9 x 10/4

Walk
17 x 4/4

W D

Dining
10 x 11/4
8' Clg.

Kitchen
9 x 13/3

10/8 x 5

B.R. #3
10/4 x 11
8' Clg.

Family Room
15 x 19
9' Clg.

B.R. #2
10 x 13
8' Clg.

Porch
26 x 6

With Garage
Width: 76'-6"
Depth: 57'-1"

Without Garage
Width: 47'-0"
Depth: 46'-0"

Plan #532-039D-0004
Price Code A

Total Living Area: 1,406 Sq. Ft.

Home has 3 bedrooms, 2 baths, 2-car detached garage and slab or crawl space foundation, please specify when ordering.

Special features

- Master bedroom has a sloped ceiling
- Kitchen and dining area merge becoming a gathering place
- Enter family room from charming covered front porch to find a fireplace and lots of windows

Plan #532-039D-0001
Price Code A

Total Living Area: 1,253 Sq. Ft.

Home has 3 bedrooms, 2 baths, 2-car garage and crawl space or slab foundation, please specify when ordering.

Special features
- Sloped ceiling and fireplace in family room add drama
- U-shaped kitchen is efficiently designed
- Large walk-in closets are found in all the bedrooms

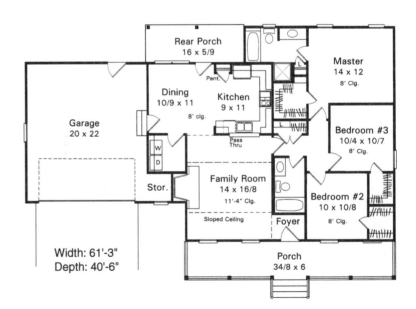

Rear Porch
16 x 5/9

Master
14 x 12
8' Clg.

Dining
10/9 x 11
8' clg.

Kitchen
9 x 11

Pant.

Garage
20 x 22

Bedroom #3
10/4 x 10/7
8' Clg.

Pass Thru

W
D

Stor.

Family Room
14 x 16/8
11'-4" Clg.

Bedroom #2
10 x 10/8
8' Clg.

Sloped Ceiling

Foyer

Width: 61'-3"
Depth: 40'-6"

Porch
34/8 x 6

LOWE'S

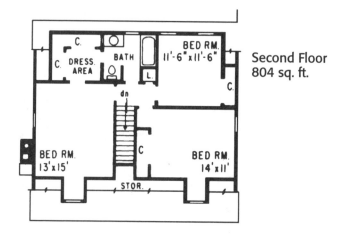

Second Floor
804 sq. ft.

BED RM.
13'x15'

BED RM.
14'x11'

DRESS.
AREA

BATH

BED RM.
11'-6" x 11'-6"

STOR.

Plan #532-008D-0178
Price Code C

Total Living Area: 1,872 Sq. Ft.

Home has 4 bedrooms, 2 baths, 2-car garage and basement foundation, drawings also include crawl space and slab foundations.

Special features

- Recessed porch has entry door with sidelights and roof dormers adding charm

- Foyer with handcrafted stair adjoins living room with fireplace

- First floor bedroom has access to bath and laundry room making it perfect for the master bedroom or a live-in parent

- Largest of three second floor bedrooms enjoys double closets and private access to hall bath

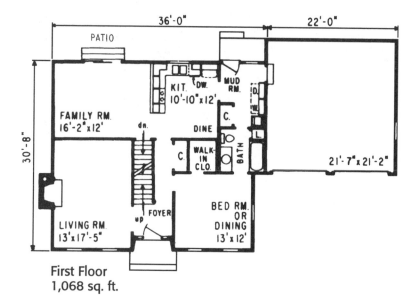

36'-0"

22'-0"

30'-8"

PATIO

FAMILY RM.
16'-2" x 12'

KIT.
10'-10" x 12'

DW.

MUD RM.

DINE

WALK-IN CLO.

BATH

21'-7" x 21'-2"

LIVING RM.
13' x 17'-5"

FOYER

BED RM.
OR
DINING
13' x 12'

First Floor
1,068 sq. ft.

Plan #532-025D-0002
Price Code A

Total Living Area: 1,397 Sq. Ft.

Home has 3 bedrooms, 2 baths and slab foundation.

Special features

- Decorative ceiling in formal dining room adds excitement to the exterior
- Bedroom #3 is highlighted by a charming window seat
- Eating bar in breakfast area provides additional space

Plan #532-020D-0007
Price Code C

Total Living Area: 1,828 Sq. Ft.

Home has 4 bedrooms, 2 baths, 2-car garage and slab foundation, drawings also include crawl space and basement foundations.

Special features

- Energy efficient home with 2" x 6" exterior walls
- Master bath features a giant walk-in closet and built-in linen storage with convenient access to utility room
- Kitchen has a unique design that is elegant and practical

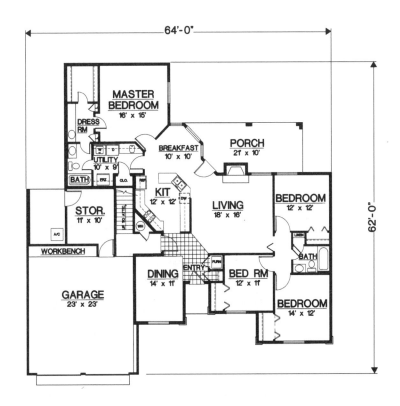

LOWE'S

Plan #532-020D-0015
Price Code AA

Total Living Area: 1,191 Sq. Ft.

Home has 3 bedrooms, 2 baths, 2-car side entry garage and slab foundation, drawings also include crawl space foundation.

Special features

- Energy efficient home with 2" x 6" exterior walls
- Master bedroom is located near living areas for maximum convenience
- Living room has a cathedral ceiling and stone fireplace

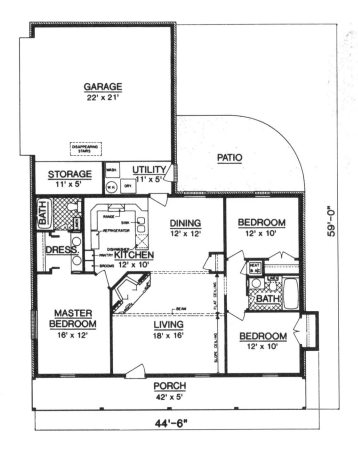

GARAGE
22' x 21'

DISAPPEARING STAIRS

PATIO

STORAGE
11' x 5'

WASH.
W. H. DRY.

UTILITY
11' x 5'

BATH

RANGE

SINK

DINING
12' x 12'

BEDROOM
12' x 10'

DISHWASHER
REFRIGERATOR

DRESS.

PANTRY
BROOMS

KITCHEN
12' x 10'

HEAT & AC

BATH

BEAM

FLAT CEILING

MASTER BEDROOM
16' x 12'

LIVING
18' x 16'

SLOPE CEILING

BEDROOM
12' x 10'

PORCH
42' x 5'

44'-6"

59'-0"

Plan #532-011D-0001
Price Code C
Total Living Area: 1,275 Sq. Ft.

Home has 3 bedrooms, 2 baths, 2-car garage and crawl space foundation.

Special features
- The kitchen expands into the dining area with the help of a center island
- Decorative columns keep the living area open to other areas
- Covered front porch adds charm to the entry

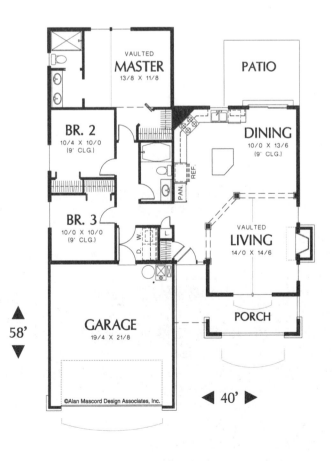

Plan #532-008D-0011
Price Code B

Total Living Area: 1,550 Sq. Ft.

Home has 3 bedrooms, 2 baths, 2-car side entry garage and basement foundation, drawings also include crawl space and slab foundations.

Special features

- Convenient mud room between the garage and kitchen
- Oversized dining area allows plenty of space for entertaining
- Master bedroom has a private bath and ample closet space
- Large patio off the family room brings the outdoors in

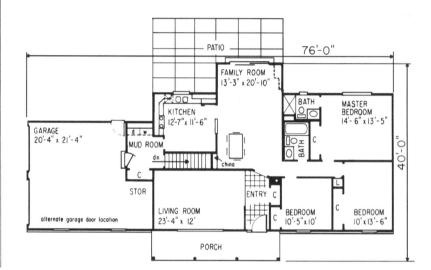

Plan #532-020D-0014
Price Code AA
Total Living Area: 1,150 Sq. Ft.

Home has 2 bedrooms, 2 baths, 2-car garage and slab foundation, drawings also include crawl space foundation.

Special features
- Bedroom with attached sitting area would make a nice master bedroom
- Living and dining rooms have 11' high box ceilings
- Ornate trimwork accents the wood sided exterior

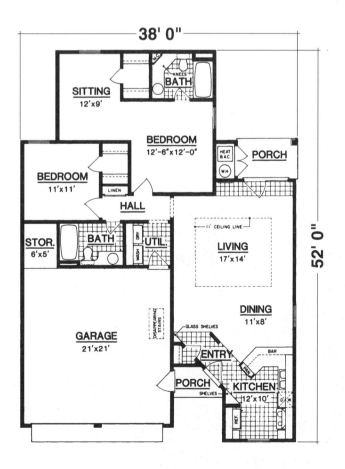

Plan #532-020D-0003
Price Code A

Total Living Area: 1,420 Sq. Ft.

Home has 3 bedrooms, 2 baths, 2-car garage and slab foundation, drawings also include crawl space foundation.

Special features

- Energy efficient home with 2" x 6" exterior walls
- Living room has a 12' ceiling, corner fireplace and atrium doors leading to the covered porch
- Secluded master suite has a garden bath and walk-in closet

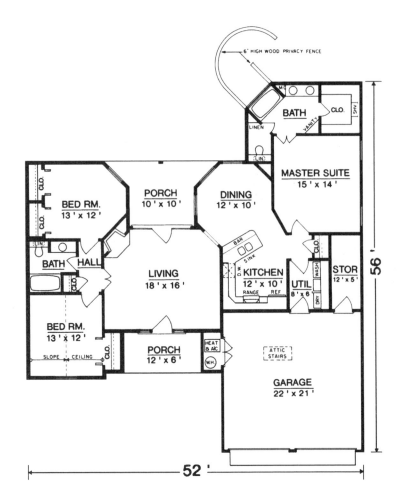

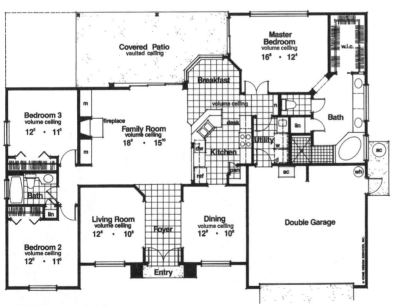

Width: 60'-0"
Depth: 45'-0"

Plan #532-047D-0020
Price Code B
Total Living Area: 1,783 Sq. Ft.

Home has 3 bedrooms, 2 baths, 2-car garage and slab foundation.

Special features
- Formal living and dining rooms in the front of the home
- Kitchen overlooks breakfast area
- Conveniently located laundry area near kitchen and master bedroom

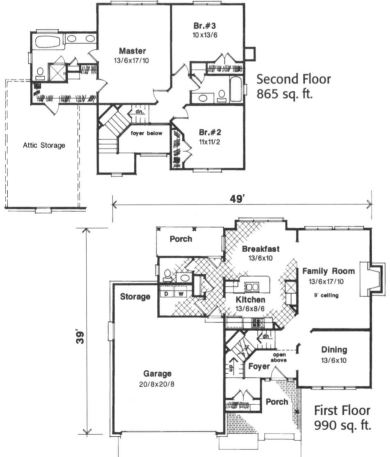

Master 13/6x17/10

Br.#3 10 x13/6

Second Floor 865 sq. ft.

Attic Storage

dn.

foyer below

Br.#2 11x11/2

49'

Porch

Breakfast 13/6x10

Family Room 13/6x17/10

9' ceiling

Storage

D W

Kitchen 13/6x8/6

dh

39'

Garage 20/8x20/8

open above

Foyer

Dining 13/6x10

Porch

First Floor 990 sq. ft.

Plan #532-039D-0015
Price Code C
Total Living Area: 1,855 Sq. Ft.

Home has 3 bedrooms, 2 1/2 baths, 2-car garage and basement foundation.

Special features
- Angled stairs add character to the two-story foyer
- Secluded dining area is formal and elegant
- Sunny master bedroom has all the luxuries
- A half bath is conveniently located off the kitchen and breakfast area

Breathtaking Balcony Overlook

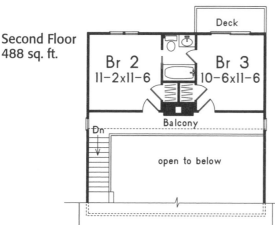

Second Floor
488 sq. ft.

Deck

Br 2
11-2x11-6

Br 3
10-6x11-6

Balcony

Dn

open to below

P

Total L

Home ha   crawl
space foun   also include
slab found

Special features

- ◼ Convenient storage for skis, etc. is located outside the front entrance
- ◼ The kitchen and dining room receive light from the box-bay window
- ◼ Large vaulted living room features a cozy fireplace and overlook from the second floor balcony
- ◼ Two second floor bedrooms share a Jack and Jill bath
- ◼ Second floor balcony extends over the entire length of the living room below

28'-0"

46'-0"

Deck

Stor

R

Br 1
9-11x11-6

Kit
10-7x
8-3

D
W

Din
10-10x
7-3

Living
23-10x12-3

Up

First Floor
811 sq. ft.

Deck

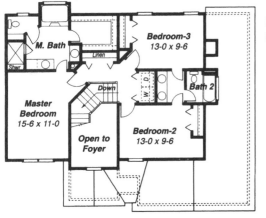

Second Floor
886 sq. ft.

M. Bath

Linen

Bedroom-3
13-0 x 9-6

Down

W
D

Bath 2

Master
Bedroom
15-6 x 11-0

Open to
Foyer

Bedroom-2
13-0 x 9-6

Plan #532-052D-0028
Price Code B

Total Living Area: 1,683 Sq. Ft.

Home has 3 bedrooms, 2 1/2 baths, 2-car garage and walk-out basement foundation.

Special features
- Open foyer and angled stairs add drama to entry
- Rear living area is open and spacious
- Master bath features garden tub, double vanities and a private toilet area

---

First Floor
797 sq. ft.

Sun Deck
16-0 x 12-0

12-0

bw

Breakfast
8-0 x 9-6

Kitchen
9-4 x 11-8

Living Area
18-0 x 11-8

Storage

Ref

Pantry

Down

34-0

Dining
11-0 x 13-4

Coats

Open Foyer

Double Garage
19-8 x 21-4

Lav

Porch

© 1996, Jannis Vann & Associates, Inc.

44-0

Second Floor
533 sq. ft.

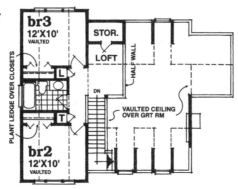

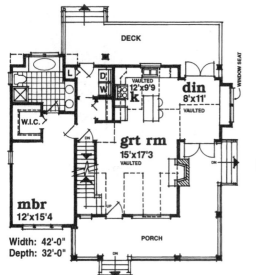

First Floor
1,050 sq. ft.

Width: 42'-0"
Depth: 32'-0"

Plan #532-062D-0055
Price Code B

Total Living Area: 1,583 Sq. Ft.

Home has 3 bedrooms, 2 baths and basement or crawl space foundation, please specify when ordering.

Special features

- Energy efficient home with 2" x 6" exterior walls
- Open kitchen includes preparation island
- Wrap-around railed porch and rear deck expand the living space to outdoor entertaining

Plan #532-028D-0003
Price Code B

Total Living Area: 1,716 Sq. Ft.

Home has 3 bedrooms, 2 baths, 2-car detached garage and crawl space or slab foundation, please specify when ordering.

Special features

- Great room boasts a fireplace and access to the kitchen/breakfast area through a large arched opening

- Master bedroom includes a huge walk-in closet and French doors that lead onto an L-shaped porch

- Bedrooms #2 and #3 share a bath and linen closet

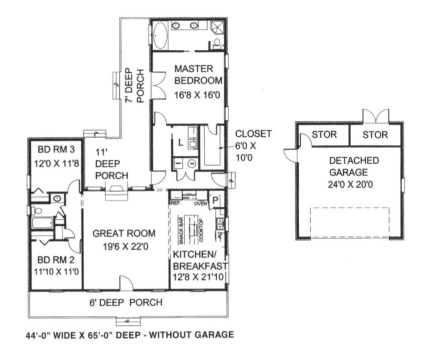

44'-0" WIDE X 65'-0" DEEP - WITHOUT GARAGE

Plan #532-008D-0094
Price Code A

Total Living Area: 1,364 Sq. Ft.

Home has 3 bedrooms, 2 baths, optional 2-car garage and basement foundation, drawings also include crawl space foundation.

Special features

- Master bedroom features a spacious walk-in closet and private bath
- Living room is highlighted with several windows
- Kitchen with snack bar is adjacent to the dining area
- Plenty of storage space throughout

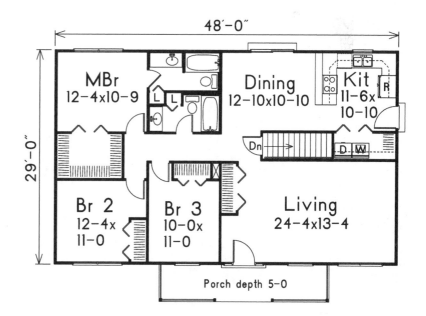

48'-0"

29'-0"

MBr
12-4x10-9

Dining
12-10x10-10

Kit
11-6x
10-10

R

Dn

D W

Br 2
12-4x
11-0

Br 3
10-0x
11-0

Living
24-4x13-4

Porch depth 5-0

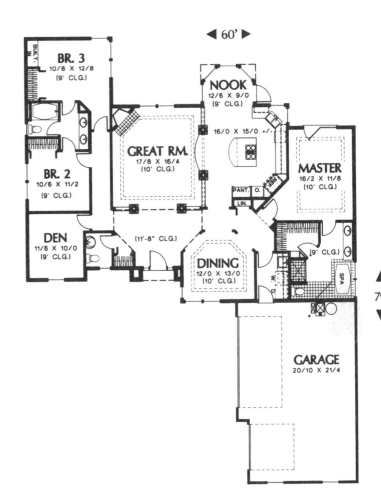

Plan #532-011D-0011
Price Code C

Total Living Area:	2,155 Sq. Ft.

Home has 3 bedrooms, 2 1/2 baths, 3-car side entry garage and crawl space foundation.

Special features

- Great room has 10' tray ceiling, corner fireplace and columns
- Well-appointed master suite features a 10' tray ceiling
- Two secondary bedrooms share a bath
- Secluded den makes an ideal home office

Plan #532-025D-0013
Price Code B
Total Living Area: 1,686 Sq. Ft.

Home has 3 bedrooms, 2 baths, 2-car side entry garage and slab foundation.

Special features
- Secondary bedrooms are separate from master suite maintaining privacy
- Island in kitchen is ideal for food preparation
- Dramatic foyer leads to great room
- Covered side porch has direct access into great room

Optional Second Floor

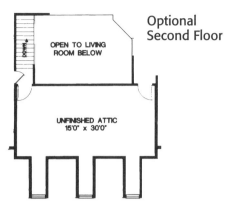

OPEN TO LIVING ROOM BELOW

UNFINISHED ATTIC
15'0" x 30'0"

First Floor
2,123 sq. ft.

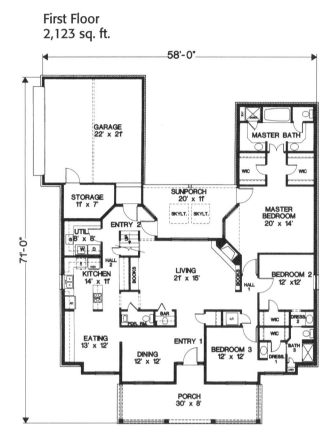

58'-0"

71'-0"

GARAGE
22' x 21'

MASTER BATH

WIC WIC

STORAGE
11' x 7'

SUNPORCH
20' x 11'

SKYLT. SKYLT.

MASTER BEDROOM
20' x 14'

UTIL
8' x 8'

W D

ENTRY 2

HALL 2

BOOKS

LIVING
21' x 15'

BOOKS

HALL 1

BEDROOM 2
12' x 12'

KITCHEN
14' x 11'

BAR

WIC DRESS 2

EATING
13' x 12'

POR. RM.

ENTRY 1

A/C

WIC

DINING
12' x 12'

BEDROOM 3
12' x 12'

DRESS 1 BATH 3

PORCH
30' x 8'

Plan #532-020D-0009
Price Code E

Total Living Area: 2,123 Sq. Ft.

Home has 3 bedrooms, 2 1/2 baths, 2-car side entry garage and crawl space foundation, drawings also include slab and basement foundations.

Special features

- Energy efficient home with 2" x 6" exterior walls
- Living room has wood burning fireplace, built-in bookshelves and a wet bar
- Skylights make the sunporch bright and comfortable
- Unfinished attic has an additional 450 square feet of living area

Width: 52'-8"
Depth: 41'-8"

DIN
10' x 12'8

Laun

Entry

FAM RM
19'2 x 13'6

KIT
11' x 10'10

GARAGE
21'4 x 21'4

DIN RM
10'8 x 11'6

LIV RM
12'4 x 15'4

Two-Story
FOYER

Covered Entry

First Floor
1,100 sq. ft.

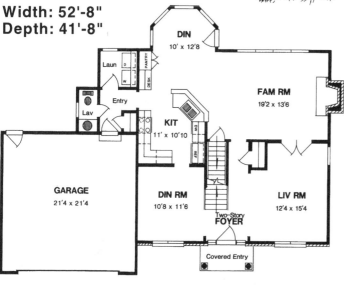

Plan #532-034D-0019
Price Code C

Total Living Area: 1,992 Sq. Ft.

Home has 4 bedrooms, 2 1/2 baths, 2-car garage and basement foundation.

Special features

- Sunny family room has lots of windows and a large fireplace
- Octagon-shaped dining area is adjacent to the kitchen for easy access
- Formal living room is separated from family room by French doors
- Master bedroom has a private bath with dressing area and walk-in closet

BR3
10'4 x 11'11

BR2
11'8 x 9'6

MBATH

WI Closet

Dress'g

Balcony

BATH2

BR4
10'8 x 9'8

Foyer Below

MBR
12'4 x 13'6

Second Floor
892 sq. ft.

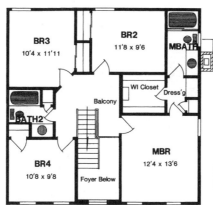

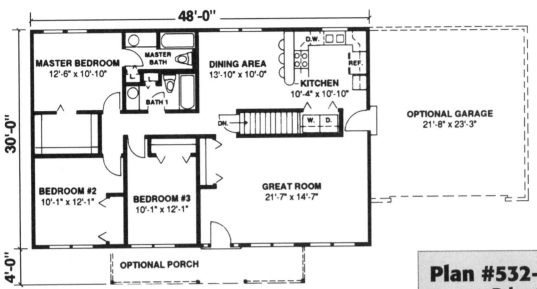

Plan #532-008D-0090
Price Code A
Total Living Area: 1,364 Sq. Ft.

Home has 3 bedrooms, 2 baths, optional 2-car garage and basement foundation.

Special features
- Bedrooms separated from living area for privacy
- Master bedroom has private bath and large walk-in closet
- Laundry area is conveniently located near kitchen
- Bright and spacious great room
- Built-in pantry in kitchen

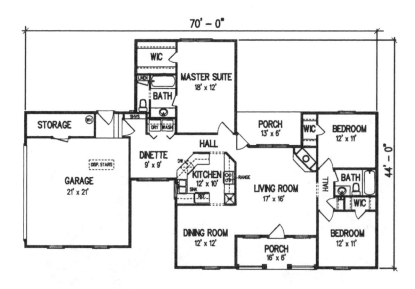

Plan #532-020D-0002
Price Code A

Total Living Area: 1,434 Sq. Ft.

Home has 3 bedrooms, 2 baths, 2-car side entry garage and crawl space foundation, drawings also include slab foundation.

Special features

- Isolated master suite for privacy includes walk-in closet and bath
- Elegant formal dining room
- Efficient kitchen has an adjacent dining area which includes shelves and access to laundry facilities
- Extra storage in garage

Plan #532-008D-0145
Price Code B

Total Living Area: 1,750 Sq. Ft.

Home has 3 bedrooms, 2 baths and basement foundation, drawings also include crawl space and slab foundations.

Special features

- ■ The family room is brightened by floor-to-ceiling windows and sliding doors providing access to large deck
- ■ Second floor sitting area is perfect for a game room or entertaining
- ■ Kitchen includes eat-in dining area plus outdoor dining patio as a bonus
- ■ Plenty of closet and storage space throughout

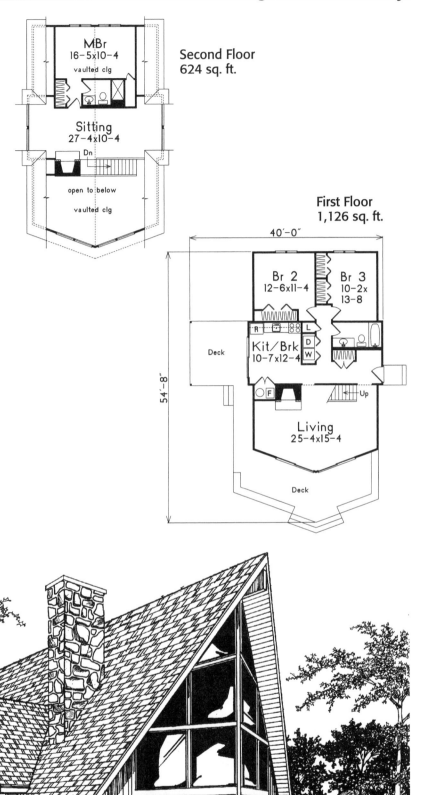

Second Floor
624 sq. ft.

MBr
16-5x10-4
vaulted clg

Sitting
27-4x10-4

Dn

open to below

vaulted clg

First Floor
1,126 sq. ft.

40'-0"

Br 2
12-6x11-4

Br 3
10-2x
13-8

Deck

Kit/Brk
10-7x12-4

54'-8"

Up

Living
25-4x15-4

Deck

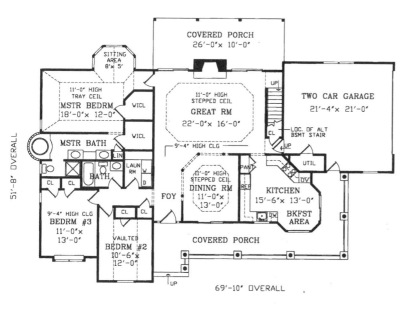

Plan #532-016D-0049
Price Code B
Total Living Area: 1,793 Sq. Ft.

Home has 3 bedrooms, 2 baths, 2-car side entry garage and basement, crawl space or slab foundation, please specify when ordering.

Special features

- Beautiful foyer leads into the great room that has a fireplace flanked by two sets of beautifully transomed doors both leading to a large covered porch

- Dramatic eat-in kitchen includes an abundance of cabinets and work-space in an exciting angled shape

- Delightful master bedroom has many amenities

- Optional bonus room above the garage has an additional 779 square feet of living area

Plan #532-026D-0122
Price Code C

Total Living Area: 1,850 Sq. Ft.

Home has 3 bedrooms, 2 baths, 2-car garage and basement foundation.

Special features

- Oversized rooms throughout
- Great room spotlights fireplace with sunny windows on both sides
- Master bedroom has private skylighted bath
- Interesting wet bar between kitchen and dining area is an added bonus when entertaining

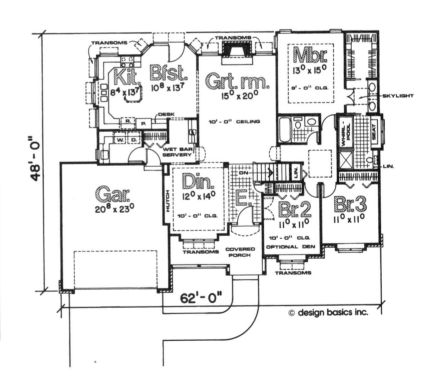

© design basics inc.

Plan #532-025D-0012
Price Code B

Total Living Area: 1,634 Sq. Ft.

Home has 3 bedrooms, 2 baths, 2-car garage and slab foundation.

Special features

■ Enter the foyer to find a nice-sized dining room to the right and a cozy great room with fireplace straight ahead

■ Secluded master suite offers privacy from other bedrooms and living areas

■ Plenty of storage throughout this home

■ Future playroom on the second floor has an additional 256 square feet of living area

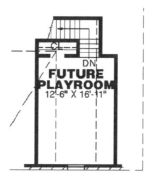

Optional
Second Floor

First Floor
1,634 sq. ft.

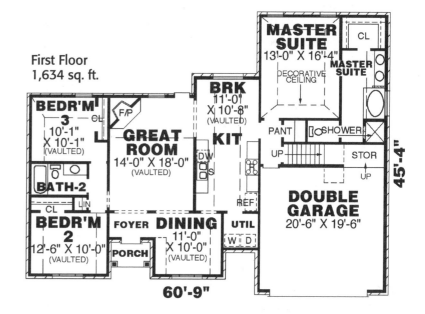

Plan #532-008D-0104
Price Code A

Total Living Area: 1,400 Sq. Ft.

Home has 2 bedrooms, 2 baths and crawl space foundation.

Special features

■ Inside and out, this home is pleasingly different

■ Activity area showcases large freestanding fireplace and spacious dining room with views

■ Laundry area is provided in a very functional kitchen

■ Master bedroom with a double-door entry is a grand bedroom with nice amenities

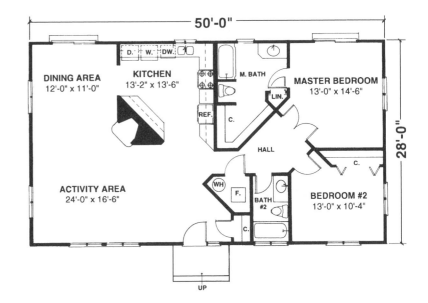

Rear View

Plan #532-049D-0008
Price Code C
Total Living Area: 1,937 Sq. Ft.

Home has 3 bedrooms, 2 baths, 2-car side entry garage and crawl space foundation.

Special features
- Upscale great room offers a sloped ceiling, fireplace with extended hearth and built-in shelves for an entertainment center

- Gourmet kitchen includes a cooktop island counter and a quaint morning room

- Master suite features a sloped ceiling, cozy sitting room, walk-in closet and a private bath with whirlpool tub

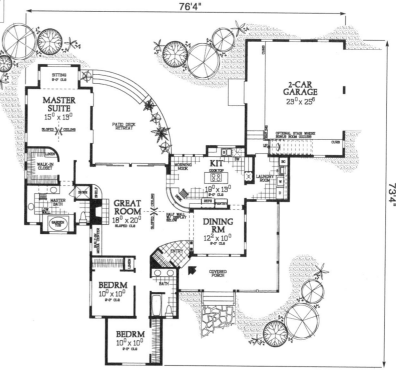

See-Through Fireplace

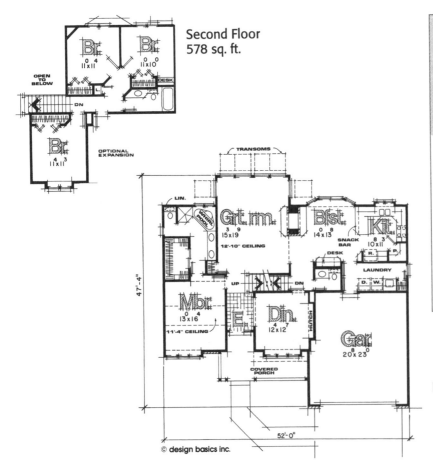

Second Floor
578 sq. ft.

First Floor
1,421 sq. ft.

© design basics inc.

Plan #532-026D-0110
Price Code C
Total Living Area: 1,999 Sq. Ft.

Home has 4 bedrooms, 2 1/2 baths, 2-car garage and basement foundation.

Special features
- Breakfast room and kitchen combine for a spacious gathering place including access to laundry area and a built-in desk area
- First floor master bedroom enjoys a private bath with a luxurious whirlpool tub
- Private dining area with unique built-in hutch adds interest

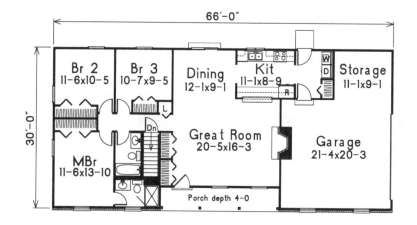

66'-0"

30'-0"

| Br 2
11-6x10-5 | Br 3
10-7x9-5 | Dining
12-1x9-1 | Kit
11-1x8-9 | Storage
11-1x9-1 |

MBr
11-6x13-10

Great Room
20-5x16-3

Garage
21-4x20-3

Porch depth 4-0

Plan #532-008D-0013
Price Code A
Total Living Area: 1,345 Sq. Ft.

Home has 3 bedrooms, 2 baths, 2-car side entry garage and basement foundation, drawings also include crawl space and slab foundations.

Special features
- Brick front details add a touch of elegance
- Master bedroom has a private full bath
- Great room combined with dining area adds spaciousness
- Garage includes handy storage area which could easily convert to a workshop space

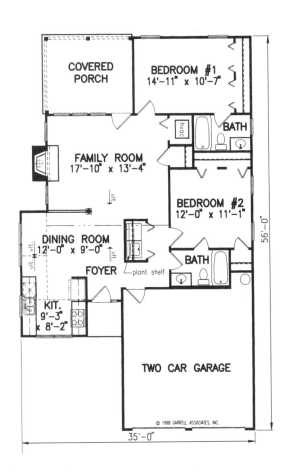

COVERED PORCH

BEDROOM #1
14'-11" x 10'-7"

BATH

FAMILY ROOM
17'-10" x 13'-4"

BEDROOM #2
12'-0" x 11'-1"

DINING ROOM
12'-0" x 9'-0"

FOYER — plant shelf

BATH

KIT.
9'-3"
x 8'-2"

56'-0"

TWO CAR GARAGE

© 1998 GARRELL ASSOCIATES, INC.

35'-0"

Plan #532-056D-0024
Price Code AA

Total Living Area: 1,093 Sq. Ft.

Home has 2 bedrooms, 2 baths, 2-car garage and slab foundation.

Special features
- Family room with fireplace over-looks large covered porch
- Vaulted family and dining rooms are adjacent to kitchen
- Bedroom #2 has its own entrance into bath
- Plant shelf accents vaulted foyer
- Centrally located laundry area

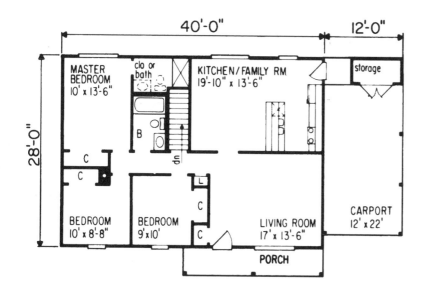

Plan #532-008D-0026
Price Code AA
Total Living Area: 1,120 Sq. Ft.

Home has 3 bedrooms, 2 baths, 1-car carport and basement foundation, drawings also include crawl space and slab foundations.

Special features
- Kitchen/family room creates a useful spacious area
- Rustic, colonial design is perfect for many surroundings
- Oversized living room is ideal for entertaining
- Carport includes a functional storage area

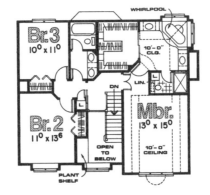

Second Floor
905 sq. ft.

First Floor
1,093 sq. ft.

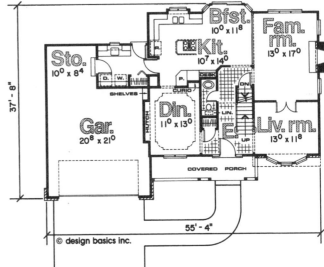

© design basics inc.

Plan #532-026D-0123
Price Code C

Total Living Area: 1,998 Sq. Ft.

Home has 3 bedrooms, 2 1/2 baths, 2-car garage and basement foundation.

Special features

- Lovely designed family room offers double-door entrance into living area
- Roomy kitchen with breakfast area is a natural gathering place
- 10' ceiling in master bedroom

TO ORDER BLUEPRINTS USE THE FORM ON PAGE 288 OR CALL TOLL-FREE **1-800-DREAM HOME** (373-2646)

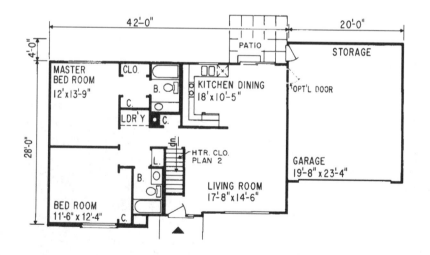

Plan #532-008D-0103
Price Code AA

Total Living Area: 1,128 Sq. Ft.

Home has 2 bedrooms, 2 baths, 2-car garage and basement foundation.

Special features

- Large living room borrows from dining area creating an expansive space
- Well-arranged U-shaped kitchen has lots of counter and cabinet storage space
- Double closets and a full bath accompany the spacious master bedroom
- Oversized garage with ample storage has door to rear patio that leads to dining area

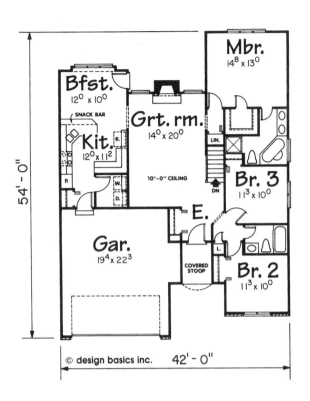

Bfst.
12⁰ x 10⁰

SNACK BAR

Kit.
12⁰ x 11²

Grt. rm.
14⁰ x 20⁰

10'-0" CEILING

Mbr.
14⁸ x 13⁰

LIN.

DN

Br. 3
11³ x 10⁰

E.

Gar.
19⁴ x 22³

COVERED STOOP

Br. 2
11³ x 10⁰

54' - 0"

42' - 0"

© design basics inc.

Plan #532-026D-0154
Price Code A

Total Living Area: 1,392 Sq. Ft.

Home has 3 bedrooms, 2 baths, 2-car garage and basement foundation.

Special features
- Centralized great room welcomes guests with a warm fireplace
- Master bedroom has a separate entrance for added privacy
- Kitchen includes breakfast room, snack counter and laundry area

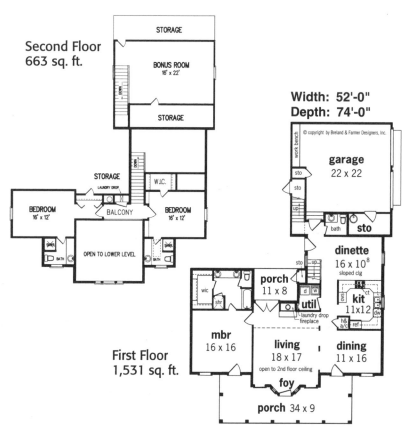

Second Floor
663 sq. ft.

First Floor
1,531 sq. ft.

Width: 52'-0"
Depth: 74'-0"

Plan #532-020D-0010
Price Code C
Total Living Area: 2,194 Sq. Ft.

Home has 3 bedrooms, 3 1/2 baths, 2-car side entry garage and crawl space foundation, drawings also include slab and basement foundations.

Special features

- Energy efficient home with 2" x 6" exterior walls

- Utility room has laundry drop conveniently located next to kitchen

- Both second floor bedrooms have large closets and their own bath

Plan #532-024D-0002
Price Code A

Total Living Area: 1,405 Sq. Ft.

Home has 3 bedrooms, 2 baths and slab foundation.

Special features

- Compact design has all the luxuries of a larger home
- Master bedroom has its privacy away from other bedrooms
- Living room has corner fireplace, access to the outdoors and easily reaches the dining area and kitchen
- Large utility room has access to the outdoors

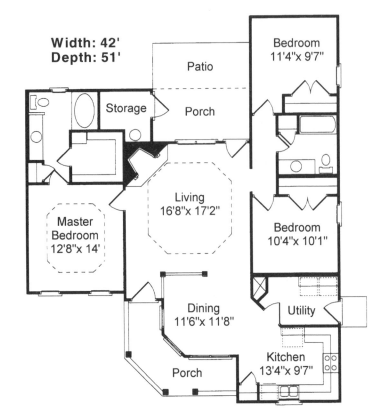

Width: 42'
Depth: 51'

Patio

Storage

Porch

Bedroom
11'4"x 9'7"

Living
16'8"x 17'2"

Master
Bedroom
12'8"x 14'

Bedroom
10'4"x 10'1"

Dining
11'6"x 11'8"

Utility

Porch

Kitchen
13'4"x 9'7"

Plan #532-011D-0005
Price Code C
Total Living Area: 1,467 Sq. Ft.

Home has 3 bedrooms, 2 baths, 2-car garage and crawl space foundation.

Special features
- Vaulted ceilings, an open floor plan and a wealth of windows create an inviting atmosphere
- Efficiently arranged kitchen has an island with built-in cooktop and a snack counter
- Plentiful storage and closet space throughout this home

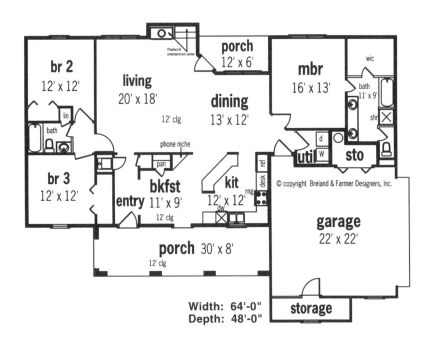

Plan #532-020D-0005
Price Code B

Total Living Area: 1,770 Sq. Ft.

Home has 3 bedrooms, 2 baths, 2-car side entry garage and slab foundation, drawings also include crawl space foundation.

Special features

- Open floor plan makes this home feel spacious
- 12' ceilings in kitchen, living, breakfast and dining areas
- Kitchen is the center of activity with views into all gathering places

Width: 64'-0"
Depth: 48'-0"

© copyright Breland & Farmer Designers, Inc.

Second Floor
848 sq. ft.

MBR
16'6 x 13'6

M.BATH

BATH 2

WI Closet

HALL

BR3
10'8 x 10'

BR2
11'4 x 10'10

Plan #532-034D-0015
Price Code C

Total Living Area: 1,868 Sq. Ft.

Home has 3 bedrooms, 2 1/2 baths, 2-car garage and basement foundation.

Special features

- Open floor plan creates an airy feeling

- Secluded study makes an ideal home office

- Large master bedroom has luxurious private bath with a walk-in closet

- Formal dining room has convenient access to kitchen

First Floor
1,020 sq. ft.

Gas fpl

GREAT RM
16'8 x 13'6

DIN
11'8 x 10'2

Laun

WI Closet

STUDY
10'6 x 9'8

KIT
11'4 x 11'6

REF

PANTRY

FOYER

LAV

GARAGE
21'4 x 21'4

DIN RM
11'4 x 10'8

Covered Porch

Width: 52'-8"
Depth: 34'-0"

Plan #532-043D-0005
Price Code B

Total Living Area: 1,734 Sq. Ft.

Home has 3 bedrooms, 2 baths, 2-car garage and crawl space foundation.

Special features

- Large entry boasts a coffered ceiling and display niches
- Sunken great room has 10' ceiling
- Kitchen island includes an eating counter
- 9' ceiling in the master bedroom
- Master bath features a corner tub and double sinks

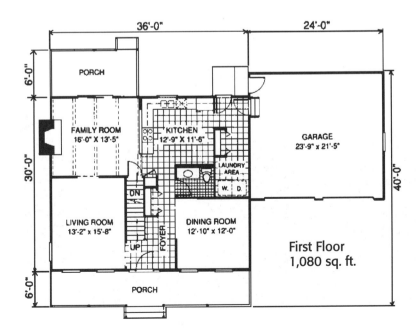

BEDROOM
12'-6" x 12'-10"

MASTER
BEDROOM
13'-4" x 15'-0"

DN

BEDROOM
15'-2" x 11'-7"

Second Floor
868 sq. ft.

PORCH

FAMILY ROOM
16'-0" X 13'-5"

KITCHEN
12'-9" X 11'-6"

GARAGE
23'-9" x 21'-5"

LAUNDRY
AREA

W. D.

DN

LIVING ROOM
13'-2" x 15'-8"

FOYER

DINING ROOM
12'-10" x 12'-0"

UP

PORCH

36'-0"

24'-0"

6'-0"

30'-0"

40'-0"

6'-0"

First Floor
1,080 sq. ft.

Plan #532-008D-0097
Price Code C

Total Living Area: 1,948 Sq. Ft.

Home has 3 bedrooms, 2 1/2 baths, 2-car garage and basement foundation, drawings also include crawl space foundation.

Special features

- Large elongated porch for moonlit evenings
- Stylish family room features beamed ceiling
- Skillfully designed kitchen is convenient to an oversized laundry area
- Second floor bedrooms are all generously sized

Plan #532-039D-0019
Price Code C

Total Living Area: 2,009 Sq. Ft.

Home has 3 bedrooms, 2 baths, 2-car side entry garage and basement foundation.

Special features

- Enter home and find large family room with fireplace flanked by double windows
- Cheerful breakfast area has access to skylighted porch
- Elegant dining area includes a built-in china cabinet
- Optional bonus room above the garage has an additional 332 square feet of living area

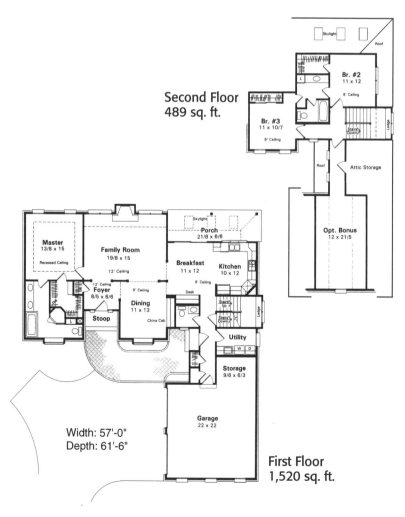

Second Floor
489 sq. ft.

Br. #2
11 x 12
8' Ceiling

Br. #3
11 x 10/7
8' Ceiling

Skylight
Roof

Stairs Down
Ledge

Roof

Attic Storage

Opt. Bonus
12 x 21/5

Master
13/8 x 15
Recessed Ceiling

Family Room
19/8 x 15
12' Ceiling

Skylight

Porch
21/8 x 6/6

Breakfast
11 x 12
9' Ceiling

Kitchen
10 x 12

Desk

12' Ceiling
Foyer
8/5 x 6/6

9' Ceiling

Dining
11 x 13

China Cab.

Stairs Up
Stairs Down
Ledge

Stoop

Utility
W D

Storage
9/6 x 6/3

Garage
22 x 22

Width: 57'-0"
Depth: 61'-6"

First Floor
1,520 sq. ft.

Plan #532-008D-0168
Price Code AA
Total Living Area: 1,092 Sq. Ft.

Home has 2 bedrooms, 2 baths, 2-car garage and basement, crawl space or slab foundation, please specify when ordering.

Special features

- Large living room is open to a U-shaped kitchen/dining area which accesses rear patio through double sliding doors

- Master bedroom has two large closets which lead to private bath

- The two-car garage has ample storage space and also accesses the rear patio

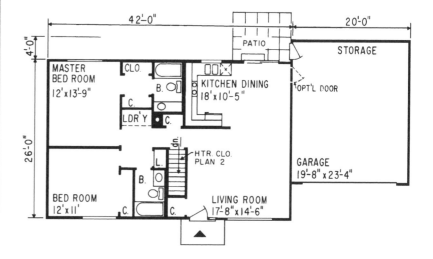

Plan #532-028D-0004
Price Code B

Total Living Area: 1,785 Sq. Ft.

Home has 3 bedrooms, 3 baths, 2-car detached garage and basement, crawl space or slab foundation, please specify when ordering.

Special features

- 9' ceilings throughout home
- Luxurious master bath includes a whirlpool tub and separate shower
- Cozy breakfast area is convenient to kitchen

COMES WITH DETACHED GARAGE PLAN.

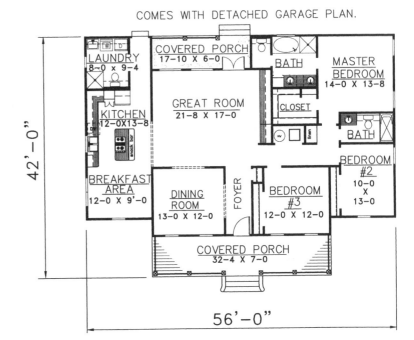

Plan #532-035D-0032
Price Code C

Total Living Area: 1,856 Sq. Ft.

Home has 3 bedrooms, 2 baths, 2-car side entry garage and walk-out basement, crawl space or slab foundation, please specify when ordering.

Special features

- Beautiful covered porch creates a Southern accent
- Kitchen has an organized feel with lots of cabinetry
- Large foyer has a grand entrance and leads into family room through columns and an arched opening

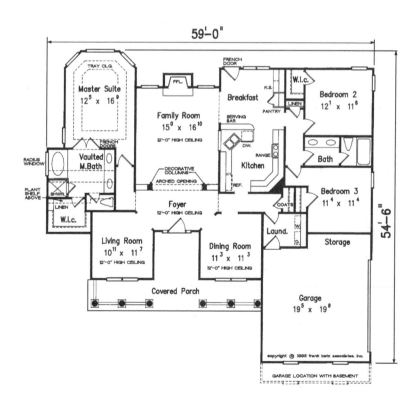

Second Floor
829 sq. ft.

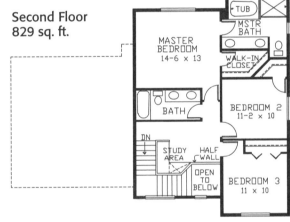

Plan #532-043D-0009
Price Code B
Total Living Area: 1,751 Sq. Ft.

Home has 3 bedrooms, 2 1/2 baths, 2-car garage and crawl space foundation.

Special features
- Charming covered front porch
- Elegant two-story entry
- Beautifully designed great room with fireplace opens to kitchen
- Large eating counter and walk-in pantry
- Second floor study area perfect for a growing family

First Floor
922 sq. ft.

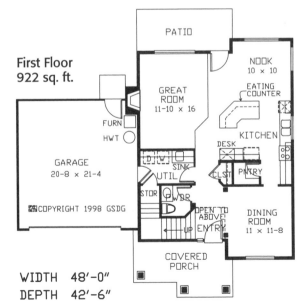

WIDTH   48'-0"
DEPTH   42'-6"

Second Floor
519 sq. ft.

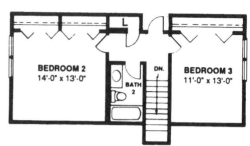

Plan #532-008D-0076
Price Code C

Total Living Area: 1,922 Sq. Ft.

Home has 3 bedrooms, 2 1/2 baths and basement foundation.

Special features

- Master bedroom includes many luxuries such as an oversized private bath and large walk-in closet

- Kitchen is spacious with a functional eat-in breakfast bar and is adjacent to nook ideal as a breakfast room

- Plenty of storage is featured in both bedrooms on the second floor and in the hall

- Enormous utility room is centrally located on the first floor

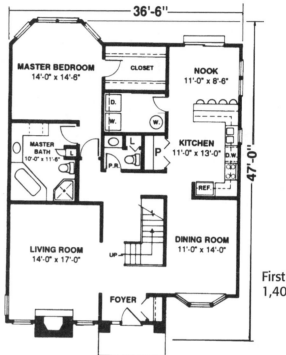

First Floor
1,403 sq. ft.

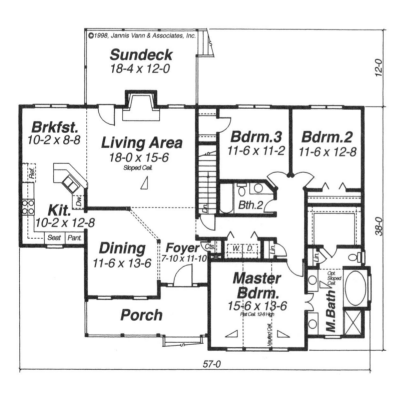

©1998, Jannis Vann & Associates, Inc.

Sundeck
18-4 x 12-0

12-0

Brkfst.
10-2 x 8-8

Living Area
18-0 x 15-6
Sloped Ceil.

Bdrm.3
11-6 x 11-2

Bdrm.2
11-6 x 12-8

Kit.
10-2 x 12-8

Seat | Pant.

Bth.2

Dining
11-6 x 13-6

Foyer
7-10 x 11-10

W. D.

Master Bdrm.
15-6 x 13-6
Flat Ceil. 12-8 High

M.Bath

Opt. Sloped Ceil.

Vaulted Ceil.

Porch

57-0

38-0

Plan #532-052D-0036
Price Code B

Total Living Area: 1,772 Sq. Ft.

Home has 3 bedrooms, 2 baths, 3-car drive under garage and basement foundation.

Special features

- Dramatic palladian window and scalloped porch are attention grabbers

- Island kitchen sink allows for easy access and views into the living and breakfast areas

- Washer and dryer closet is easily accessible from all bedrooms

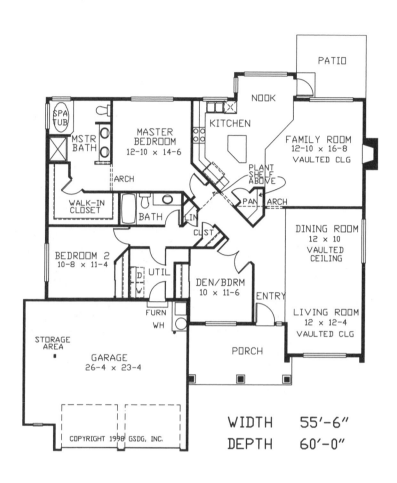

PATIO

NOOK

KITCHEN

SPA TUB

MSTR BATH

MASTER BEDROOM
12-10 x 14-6

FAMILY ROOM
12-10 x 16-8
VAULTED CLG

PLANT SHELF ABOVE

ARCH

WALK-IN CLOSET

BATH

PAN ARCH

LIN

DINING ROOM
12 x 10
VAULTED CEILING

CUST

BEDROOM 2
10-8 x 11-4

UTIL

DEN/BDRM
10 x 11-6

ENTRY

D W

FURN

WH

LIVING ROOM
12 x 12-4
VAULTED CLG

STORAGE AREA

GARAGE
26-4 x 23-4

PORCH

COPYRIGHT 1998 GSDG, INC.

WIDTH 55'-6"
DEPTH 60'-0"

Plan #532-043D-0003
Price Code C
Total Living Area: 1,890 Sq. Ft.

Home has 3 bedrooms, 2 baths, 2-car garage and crawl space foundation.

Special features
- Inviting covered porch
- Vaulted ceilings in living, dining and family rooms
- Kitchen is open to family room and nook
- Large walk-in pantry in kitchen
- Arch accented master bath has spa tub, double sinks and walk-in closet

48'0"

59'0"

RAILING

COVERED
PORCH
RETREAT

GREAT
ROOM
17⁰ x 16⁴
SLOPED CEILING

MASTER
SUITE
12⁶ x 14²
SLOPED CLG

SHELF

LOW WALL

PLANT SHELF ABOVE

KIT
10⁰ x 12²
9'-0" CLG

DN

LINEN

W

D

WALK-IN
CLOSET

SNACK BAR

BATH

LAUNDRY

PANTRY

MASTER
BATH

GARDEN
TUB

DINING
RM
10⁰ x 11⁰
COFFERED CLG

BEDRM/
MEDIA
12⁶ x 11⁰
9'-0" CLG

FOYER

SHELF

SHWR

SHELF

COVERED
PORCH

SHELF

SLPNG   CLG

STEP

2-CAR
GARAGE
19⁸ x 21⁰

SHELF

Plan #532-049D-0012
Price Code A

Total Living Area: 1,295 Sq. Ft.

Home has 2 bedrooms, 2 baths, 2-car garage and basement foundation.

Special features
■ Wrap-around porch is a lovely place for dining

■ A fireplace gives a stunning focal point to the great room that is heightened with a sloped ceiling

■ The master suite is full of luxurious touches such as a walk-in closet and a lush private bath

Plan #532-013D-0022
Price Code C

Total Living Area: 1,992 Sq. Ft.

Home has 4 bedrooms, 3 baths, 2-car side entry garage and basement, crawl space or slab foundation, please specify when ordering.

Special features

- Interesting angled walls add drama to many of the living areas including the family room, master bedroom and breakfast area
- Covered porch includes a spa and the outdoor kitchen with sink, refrigerator and cooktop
- Enter the majestic master bath to find a dramatic corner oversized tub

Plan #532-035D-0048
Price Code C

Total Living Area: 1,915 Sq. Ft.

Home has 4 bedrooms, 3 baths, 2-car garage and walk-out basement, slab or crawl space foundation, please specify when ordering.

Special features
- Large breakfast area overlooks vaulted great room
- Master suite has cheerful sitting room and a private bath
- Plan features unique in-law suite with private bath and walk-in closet

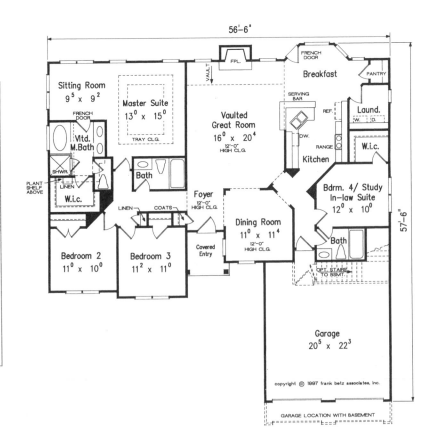

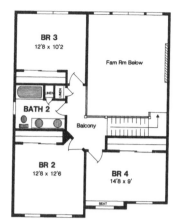

Second Floor
570 sq. ft.

Plan #532-034D-0020
Price Code C
Total Living Area: 2,018 Sq. Ft.

Home has 4 bedrooms, 2 1/2 baths, 2-car garage and basement foundation.

Special features
- Family room is situated near dining area and kitchen creating a convenient layout
- First floor master bedroom features private bath with step-up tub and bay window
- Laundry area is located on the first floor

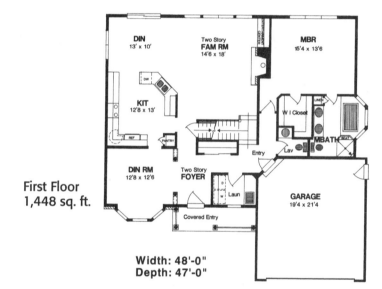

First Floor
1,448 sq. ft.

Width: 48'-0"
Depth: 47'-0"

LOWE'S

Plan #532-019D-0011
Price Code C
Total Living Area: 1,955 Sq. Ft.

Home has 3 bedrooms, 2 baths, 2-car side entry garage and crawl space foundation, drawings also include slab foundation

Special features

- Porch adds outdoor area to this design
- Dining and great rooms are visible from foyer through a series of elegant archways
- Kitchen overlooks great room and breakfast room

WIDTH 65-0

MASTER BEDRM
12-8 X 14-6
10 FT CLG

MASTER BATH
10 FT CLG

BATH 2

BEDRM 2
11-0 X 13-6

BEDRM 3
12-6 X 13-4

FOYER
10 FT CLG

DINING ROOM
12-2 X 14-0
10 FT CLG

GREAT ROOM
18-6 X 15-6
10 FT CLG

FP

BRKFST RM
12-0 X 10-0
10 FT CLG

UTIL
6-8 X 8-6

PAN

KITCHEN
12-6 X 14-0
10 FT CLG

DEPTH 58-8

PORCH

GARAGE

COPYRIGHT LARRY E. BELK

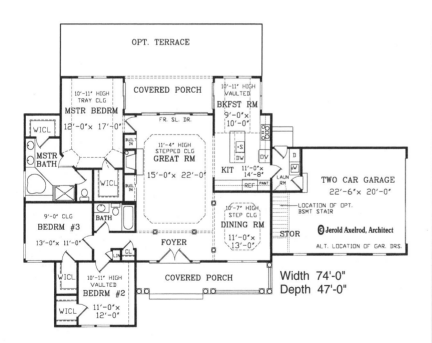

Width 74'-0"
Depth 47'-0"

Plan #532-016D-0001
Price Code D
Total Living Area: 1,783 Sq. Ft.

Home has 3 bedrooms, 2 baths, 2-car side entry garage and basement, crawl space or slab foundation, please specify when ordering.

Special features
- The front to rear flow of the great room, with built-ins on one side is a furnishing delight
- Bedrooms are all quietly zoned on one side
- The master bedroom is separated for privacy
- Every bedroom features a walk-in closet

Sundeck
14-0 x 10-0

Brkfst.
8-2 x 8-2

Kitchen
10-0 x 8-2

Dining
11-10 x 10-0

Bdrm.3
10-0 x 11-6

Master
Bdrm.
10-8 x 16-10

Living Area
13-8 x 15-0

Bdrm.2
13-6 x 11-2

M.Bath

©1998, Jannis Vann & Associates, Inc.

10-0

32-0

52-0

Plan #532-052D-0011
Price Code A
Total Living Area: 1,325 Sq. Ft.

Home has 3 bedrooms, 2 baths, 2-car drive under garage and basement or crawl space foundation, please specify when ordering.

Special features

- Sloped ceiling and a fireplace in living area creates a cozy feeling

- Formal dining and breakfast areas have an efficiently designed kitchen between them

- Master bedroom has a walk-in closet with luxurious private bath

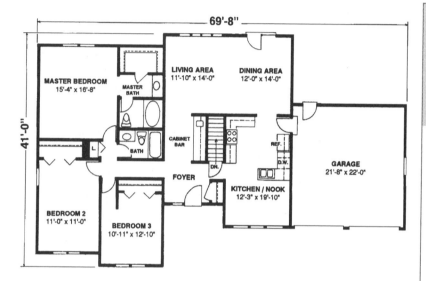

Plan #532-008D-0084
Price Code B
Total Living Area: 1,704 Sq. Ft.

Home has 3 bedrooms, 2 baths, 2-car garage and basement foundation.

Special features

- Open living and dining areas combine for added spaciousness
- Master bedroom features a private bath and walk-in closet
- Sunny kitchen/nook has space for dining
- Cabinet bar in hallway leading to living area is designed for entertaining

LOWE'S

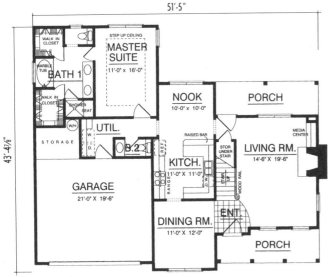

51'-5"

43'-4⅞"

WALK IN CLOSET

STEP UP CEILING

MASTER SUITE
11'-0" x 16'-0"

MARBLE TUB

BATH 1

WALK IN CLOSET

SHOWER SEAT

W/H

UTIL.

W. D.

B.2

STORAGE

REF.

NOOK
10'-0" x 10'-0"

PORCH

RAISED BAR

RANGE

KITCH.
11'-0" X 11'-0"

STOR. UNDER STAIR

STAIR UP

WOOD RAIL

MEDIA CENTER

LIVING RM.
14'-6" X 19'-6"

GARAGE
21'-0" X 19'-6"

DINING RM.
11'-0" X 12'-0"

ENT.

PORCH

First Floor
1,235 sq. ft.

OPTIONAL
BALCONY

WOOD RAIL

BED RM.4
11'-0" X 11'-0"

STAIR DOWN

WOOD RAIL

B.3

LINEN STOR.

SHELVES

BED RM.2
11'-0" X 12'-0

WALK IN CLOSET

WALK IN CLOSET

BED RM.3
11'-0" X 11'-0"

Second Floor
661 sq. ft.

Plan #532-030D-0006
Price Code C

Total Living Area: 1,896 Sq. Ft.

Home has 4 bedrooms, 2 1/2 baths, 2-car garage and basement, crawl space or slab foundation, please specify when ordering.

Special features

- Living room has lots of windows, a media center and a fireplace
- Centrally located kitchen with breakfast nook
- Extra storage in garage
- Covered porch in front and rear of home
- Optional balcony on second floor

Island Workspace

Plan #532-011D-0021
Price Code C

Total Living Area: 1,464 Sq. Ft.

Home has 3 bedrooms, 2 1/2 baths, 2-car garage and crawl space foundation.

Special features

- Contemporary styled home has a breathtaking two-story foyer and a lovely open staircase
- U-shaped kitchen is designed for efficiency
- Elegant great room has a cozy fireplace

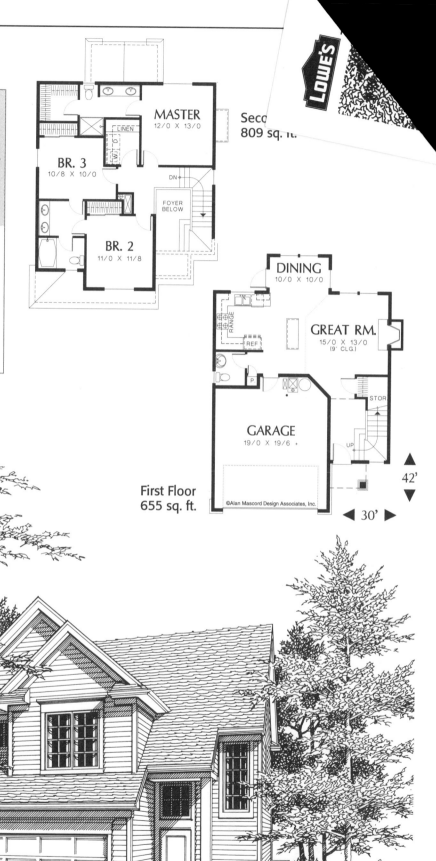

MASTER
12/0 X 13/0

BR. 3
10/8 X 10/0

LINEN

W. D

DN

FOYER BELOW

BR. 2
11/0 X 11/8

Seco
809 sq. ft.

DINING
10/0 X 10/0

RANGE

REF

GREAT RM.
15/0 X 13/0
(9' CLG.)

P

STOR

GARAGE
19/0 X 19/6

UP

First Floor
655 sq. ft.

©Alan Mascord Design Associates, Inc.

42'

30'

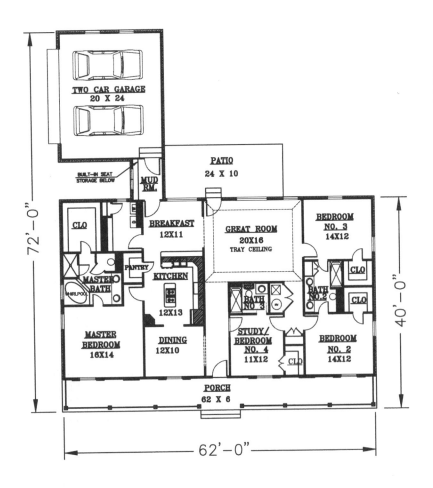

Plan #532-028D-0008
Price Code C

Total Living Area: 2,156 Sq. Ft.

Home has 4 bedrooms, 3 baths, 2-car side entry garage and basement, crawl space or slab foundation, please specify when ordering.

Special features

- Secluded master bedroom has spa-style bath with corner whirlpool tub, large shower, double sinks and a walk-in closet
- Kitchen overlooks rear patio
- Plenty of windows add an open, airy feel to the great room

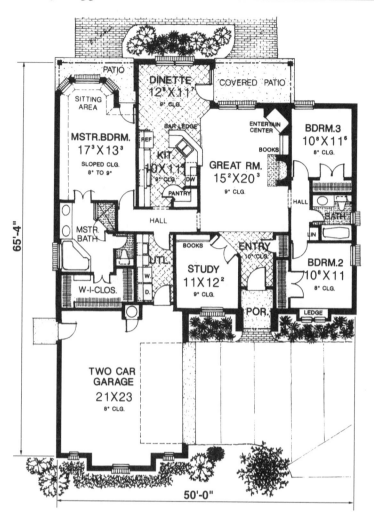

Floor plan labels:
- PATIO
- DINETTE 12⁸ X 11⁷ — 9' CLG.
- COVERED PATIO
- SITTING AREA
- MSTR. BDRM. 17³ X 13³ — SLOPED CLG. 8' TO 9'
- ENTERTAIN CENTER
- BDRM. 3 10⁶ X 11⁶ — 8' CLG.
- BAR LEDGE
- REF
- BOOKS
- KIT. 10 X 11⁵ — 9' CLG.
- DW
- GREAT RM. 15² X 20³ — 9' CLG.
- PANTRY
- HALL
- BATH
- LIN
- MSTR. BATH
- UTL
- W. D.
- BOOKS
- ENTRY 10' CLG.
- BDRM. 2 10⁶ X 11 — 8' CLG.
- W-I-CLOS.
- STUDY 11 X 12² — 9' CLG.
- POR.
- LEDGE
- TWO CAR GARAGE 21X23 — 8' CLG.
- 65'-4"
- 50'-0"

Plan #532-036D-0060
Price Code B

Total Living Area: 1,760 Sq. Ft.

Home has 3 bedrooms, 2 baths, 2-car side entry garage and slab foundation.

Special features
- Stone and brick exterior has old-world charm
- Master bedroom includes a sitting area and is situated away from other bedrooms for privacy
- Kitchen and dinette access the outdoors
- Great room includes fireplace, built-in bookshelves and an entertainment center

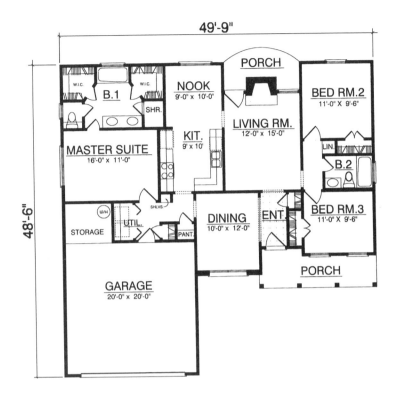

Plan #532-030D-0001
Price Code A
Total Living Area: 1,374 Sq. Ft.

Home has 3 bedrooms, 2 baths, 2-car garage and slab or crawl space foundation, please specify when ordering.

Special features
- Garage has extra storage space
- Spacious living room has fireplace
- Well-designed kitchen enjoys an adjacent breakfast nook
- Separated master suite maintains privacy

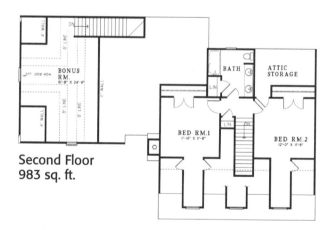

Second Floor
983 sq. ft.

First Floor
1,124 sq. ft.

Plan #532-055D-0022
Price Code C

Total Living Area: 2,107 Sq. Ft.

Home has 3 bedrooms, 2 1/2 baths, 2-car garage and walk-out basement, basement, crawl space or slab foundation, please specify when ordering.

Special features

- ■ Kitchen has pantry and adjacent dining area
- ■ Master bedroom has a bath and a large walk-in closet
- ■ Second floor bedrooms have attic storage
- ■ Bonus room above the garage has an additional 324 square feet of living area

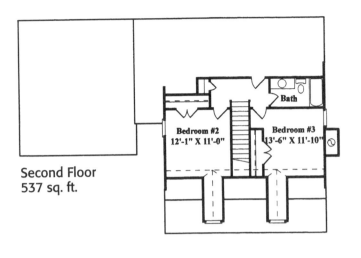

Second Floor
537 sq. ft.

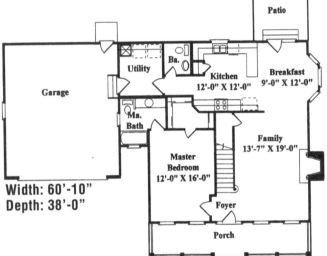

Width: 60'-10"
Depth: 38'-0"

First Floor
1,072 sq. ft.

Plan #532-024D-0007
Price Code B

Total Living Area: 1,609 Sq. Ft.

Home has 3 bedrooms, 2 1/2 baths, 2-car garage and slab foundation.

Special features

- ■ Sunny bay window in breakfast room
- ■ U-shaped kitchen with pantry
- ■ Spacious utility room
- ■ Bedrooms on second floor feature dormers
- ■ Family room includes plenty of space for entertaining

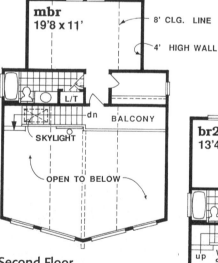

mbr
19'8 x 11'

8' CLG. LINE

4' HIGH WALL

dn   BALCONY

SKYLIGHT

OPEN TO BELOW

Second Floor
482 sq. ft.

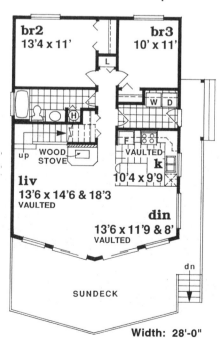

First Floor
1,061 sq. ft.

br2
13'4 x 11'

br3
10' x 11'

L

W D

H

up   WOOD
STOVE

VAULTED

k
10'4 x 9'9

liv
13'6 x 14'6 & 18'3
VAULTED

din
13'6 x 11'9 & 8'
VAULTED

dn

SUNDECK

F

Width: 28'-0"
Depth: 39'-9"

Plan #532-062D-0048
Price Code B
Total Living Area: 1,543 Sq. Ft.

Home has 3 bedrooms, 2 baths, and crawl space foundation.

Special features

- Enormous sundeck makes this a popular vacation style
- A woodstove warms the vaulted living and dining rooms
- A vaulted kitchen has a prep island and breakfast bar
- Second floor vaulted master bedroom has private bath and walk-in closet

Width: 66'-5"
Depth: 60'-0"

Porch
12/4 x 14/3
Vaulted Ceiling

Master
18 x 14
Recessed Ceiling

Breakfast
12/4 x 10/8
Desk
9' Ceiling

Br. #2
12 x 11
9' Ceiling

Family Room
20 x 15/3
11'-7" Ceiling

Kitchen
14/4 x 9/8

Utility
9/8 x 8/10

Foyer
8/8 x 11/7

Dining
13/4 x 11/7
11'-7" Ceiling

Garage
24 x 24

Br. #3
12 x 11
9' Ceiling

Porch
11/4 x 6

Plan #532-039D-0014
Price Code C

Total Living Area: 1,849 Sq. Ft.

Home has 3 bedrooms, 2 baths, 2-car garage and crawl space or slab foundation, please specify when ordering.

Special features

■ Open floor plan creates an airy feeling

■ Kitchen and breakfast area include center island, pantry and built-in desk

■ Master bedroom has a private entrance off the breakfast area and a view of the vaulted porch

COPYRIGHT LARRY E. BELK

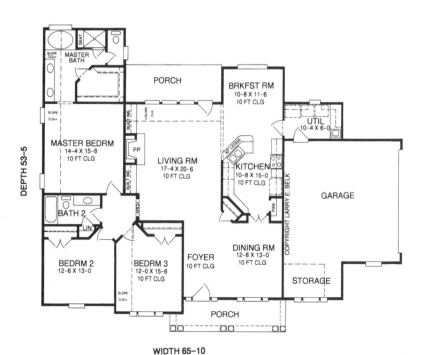

DEPTH 53-5

WIDTH 65-10

Plan #532-019D-0013
Price Code C

Total Living Area: 1,932 Sq. Ft.

Home has 3 bedrooms, 2 baths, 2-car side entry garage and crawl space foundation, drawings also include slab foundation.

Special features

- Double arches form entrance to this elegantly styled home
- Two palladian windows add distinction to facade
- Kitchen has an angled eating bar opening to the breakfast and living rooms

Plan #532-008D-0063
Price Code C

Total Living Area: 2,086 Sq. Ft.

Home has 3 bedrooms, 2 baths, 2-car garage and partial basement/crawl space foundation.

Special features

- An angled foyer leads to a vaulted living room with sunken floor
- Dining room, activity room, nook and kitchen all have vaulted ceilings
- Skillfully designed kitchen features an angled island with breakfast bar
- Master bedroom is state-of-the-art with a luxury bath and giant walk-in closet

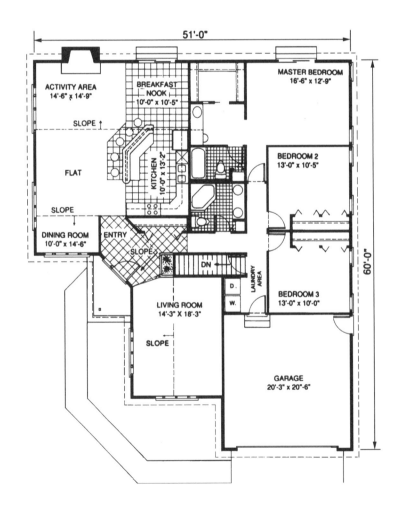

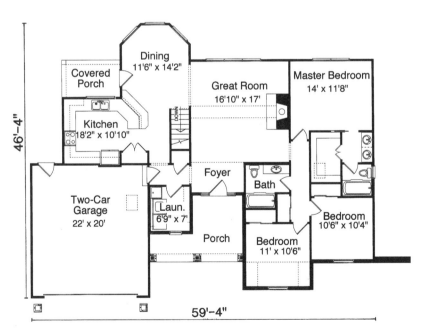

Plan #532-065D-0034
Price Code B
Total Living Area: 1,509 Sq. Ft.

Home has 3 bedrooms, 2 baths, 2-car garage and basement foundation.

Special features
- A grand opening between the great room and dining area visually expands the living space
- The kitchen is a delightful place to prepare meals with snack bar and large pantry
- Master bedroom enjoys a private bath with double-bowl vanity and large walk-in closet

Plan #532-008D-0179
Price Code C

Total Living Area: 1,973 Sq. Ft.

Home has 3 bedrooms, 2 1/2 baths, 2-car garage and partial basement/ crawl space foundation.

Special features

- This country colonial offers a grand-sized living room with views to the front and rear of home

- Living room features cozy fireplace and accesses master bedroom complete with walk-in closet and compartmented bath

- Laundry room with half bath and coat closet convenient to garage

- Second floor comprised of two large bedrooms and a full bath

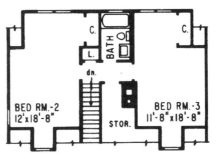

Second Floor
636 sq. ft.

First Floor
1,337 sq. ft.

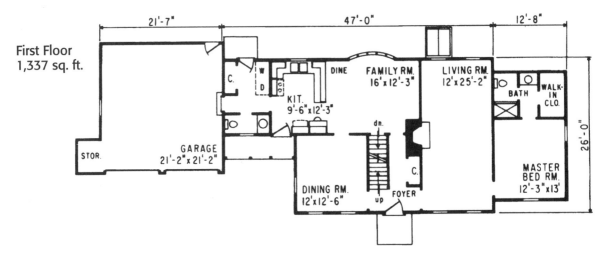

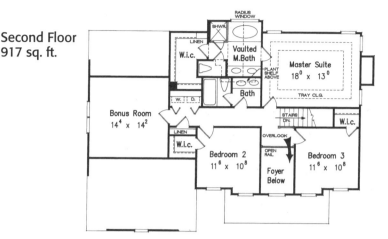

Second Floor
917 sq. ft.

Plan #532-035D-0031
Price Code C

Total Living Area: 2,052 Sq. Ft.

Home has 4 bedrooms, 3 baths, 2-car garage and walk-out basement, crawl space or slab foundation, please specify when ordering.

Special features

- Terrific family room has a fireplace and several windows adding sunlight
- Bedroom #4/study has a private bath making it an ideal in-law suite
- Bonus room on the second floor has an additional 216 square feet of living area

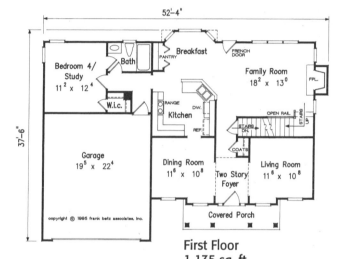

First Floor
1,135 sq. ft.

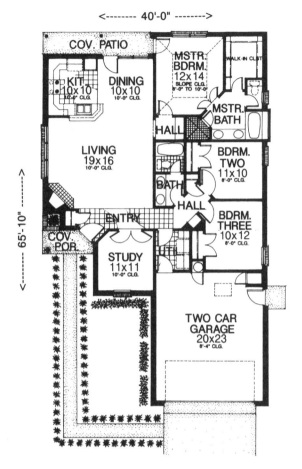

Plan #532-036D-0056
Price Code B

Total Living Area: 1,604 Sq. Ft.

Home has 3 bedrooms, 2 baths, 2-car garage and slab foundation.

Special features

- Ideal design for a narrow lot
- Living and dining areas combine for a spacious feel
- Secluded study has a double-door entry for privacy
- Master bedroom has a spacious private bath

© Michael E. Nelson
NELSON DESIGN GROUP, LL

Plan #532-055D-0051
Price Code C

Total Living Area: 1,848 Sq. Ft.

Home has 3 bedrooms, 2 baths, 2-car rear entry garage and crawl space or slab foundation, please specify when ordering.

Special features

- Kitchen is conveniently located near the dining area
- Great room has a fireplace and built-in bookshelves
- Kid's nook near laundry room includes bench with storage and hanging clothes space
- Master suite has a sitting area

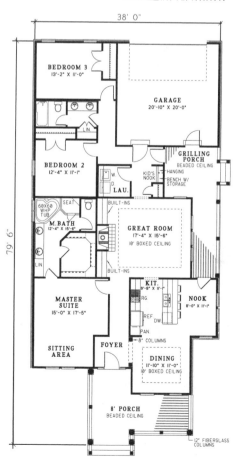

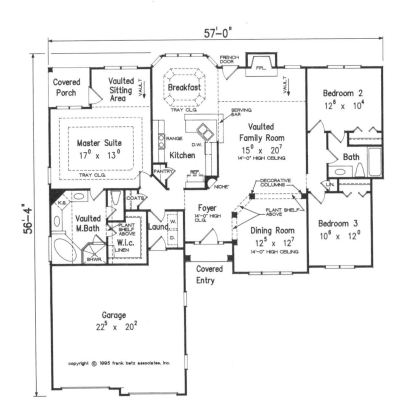

Plan #532-035D-0028
Price Code B

Total Living Area: 1,779 Sq. Ft.

Home has 3 bedrooms, 2 baths, 2-car garage and walk-out basement, slab or crawl space foundation, please specify when ordering.

Special features
- Well-designed floor plan has vaulted family room with fireplace and access to the outdoors
- Decorative columns separate the dining area from the foyer
- A vaulted ceiling adds spaciousness in master bath with walk-in closet

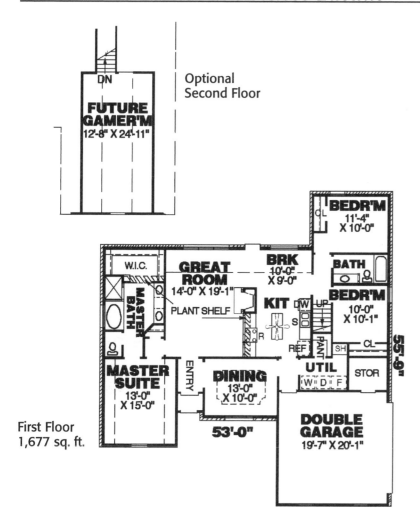

Optional
Second Floor

FUTURE GAMER'M
12'-8" X 24'-11"
DN

First Floor
1,677 sq. ft.

Plan #532-025D-0010
Price Code B

Total Living Area: 1,677 Sq. Ft.

Home has 3 bedrooms, 2 baths, 2-car side entry garage and slab foundation.

Special features

■ Master suite has a secluded feel with a private and remote location from other bedrooms

■ Great room is complete with fireplace and beautiful windows

■ Optional second floor has an additional 350 square feet of living area

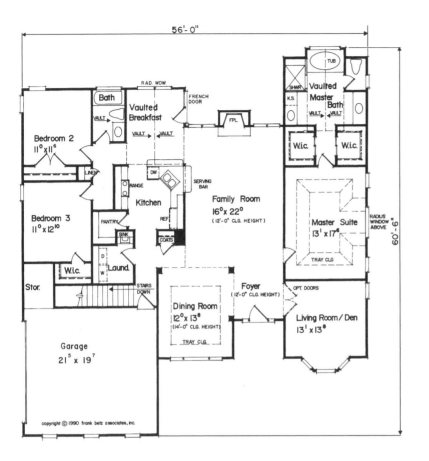

Plan #532-035D-0003
Price Code C
Total Living Area: 2,115 Sq. Ft.

Home has 3 bedrooms, 2 baths, 2-car side entry garage and walk-out basement, crawl space or slab foundation, please specify when ordering.

Special features
- Cozy living room/den has a double-door entry and makes an ideal office space
- Kitchen has serving bar which overlooks vaulted breakfast area and family room
- Master suite has all the amenities

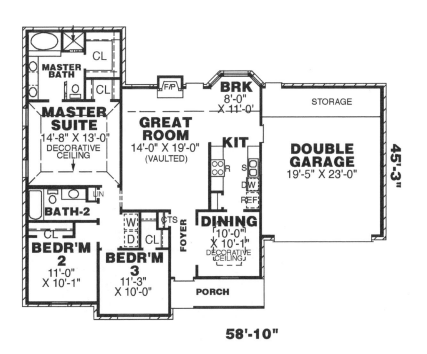

Plan #532-025D-0005
Price Code A

Total Living Area: 1,429 Sq. Ft.

Home has 3 bedrooms, 2 baths, 2-car garage and slab foundation.

Special features

- Master bedroom features a spacious private bath and double walk-in closets
- Formal dining room has convenient access to the kitchen which is perfect for entertaining
- Additional storage can be found in the garage

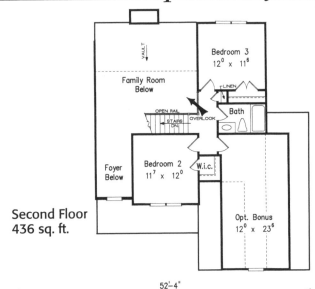

Second Floor
436 sq. ft.

Plan #532-035D-0047
Price Code C
Total Living Area: 1,818 Sq. Ft.

Home has 3 bedrooms, 2 1/2 baths, 2-car garage and walk-out basement, slab or crawl space foundation, please specify when ordering.

Special features
■ Spacious breakfast area extends into the family room and kitchen

■ Master suite has a tray ceiling and vaulted bath with walk-in closet

■ Optional bonus room above the garage has an additional 298 square feet of living area

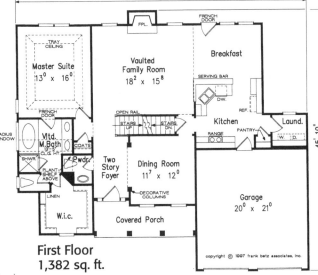

First Floor
1,382 sq. ft.

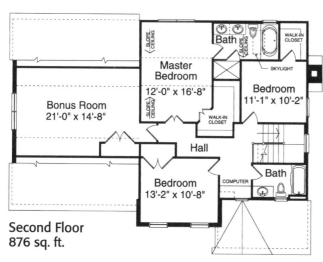

Second Floor
876 sq. ft.

Bonus Room
21'-0" x 14'-8"

Master Bedroom
12'-0" x 16'-8"

SLOPE CEILING

Bath

WALK-IN CLOSET

SKYLIGHT

Bedroom
11'-1" x 10'-2"

WALK-IN CLOSET

Hall

Bath

COMPUTER

Bedroom
13'-2" x 10'-8"

Plan #532-065D-0017
Price Code C
Total Living Area: 1,856 Sq. Ft.

Home has 3 bedrooms, 2 1/2 baths, 2-car garage and basement foundation.

Special features
- The roomy kitchen offers an abundance of cabinets and counterspace as well as a convenient pantry
- Master bedroom includes a sloped ceiling and a deluxe bath
- Bonus room on the second floor has an additional 325 square feet of living area

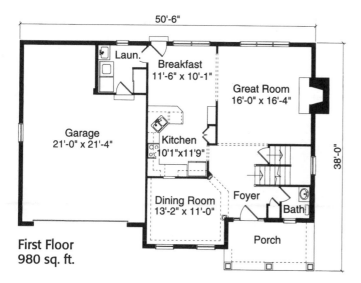

50'-6"

Laun.

Breakfast
11'-6" x 10'-1"

Great Room
16'-0" x 16'-4"

Garage
21'-0" x 21'-4"

Kitchen
10'1"x11'9"

38'-0"

Dining Room
13'-2" x 11'-0"

Foyer

Bath

Porch

First Floor
980 sq. ft.

Plan #532-030D-0002
Price Code A

Total Living Area: 1,429 Sq. Ft.

Home has 3 bedrooms, 2 baths, 2-car garage and crawl space or slab foundation, please specify when ordering.

Special features

- Master suite includes a sitting area and private bath with two walk-in closets
- Kitchen and dining area overlook the living room
- Living room has a fireplace, media center and access to the covered porch

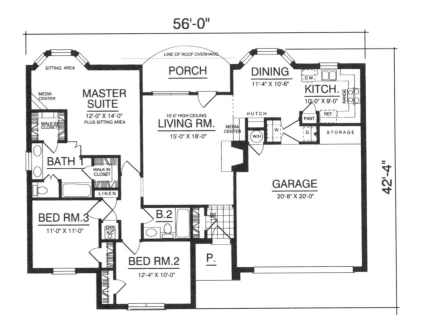

Formal And Informal Areas

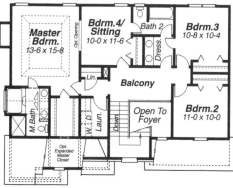

Second Floor
1,129 sq. ft.

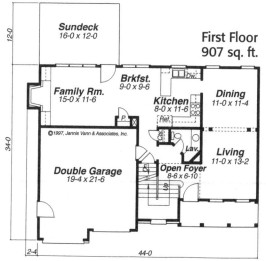

First Floor
907 sq. ft.

Plan #532-052D-0061
Price Code C

Total Living Area: 2,036 Sq. Ft.

Home has 4 bedrooms, 2 1/2 baths, 2-car garage and walk-out basement, crawl space or slab foundation, please specify when ordering.

Special features

- Stonework accents the facade giving it a European flair
- U-shaped staircase has a window lighting the foyer
- Family room and kitchen combine for added space
- Vaulted living and dining areas create a formal feel

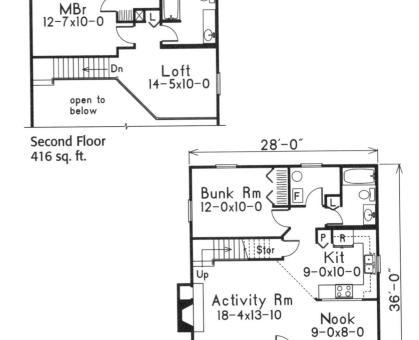

Second Floor
416 sq. ft.

First Floor
784 sq. ft.

Plan #532-008D-0072
Price Code A

Total Living Area: 1,200 Sq. Ft.

Home has 2 bedrooms, 2 baths and crawl space foundation.

Special features

- Enjoy lazy summer evenings on this magnificent porch
- Activity area has fireplace and ascending stair from cozy loft
- Kitchen features built-in pantry
- Master bedroom enjoys a large bath, walk-in closet and cozy loft overlooking room below

Plan #532-065D-0033
Price Code B
Total Living Area: 1,648 Sq. Ft.

Home has 3 bedrooms, 2 baths, 2-car garage and basement foundation.

Special features
■ A large master bedroom with 11' ceiling and access to the covered porch adds elegance

■ Open floor plan features varied ceiling heights

■ Dining area accesses covered porch

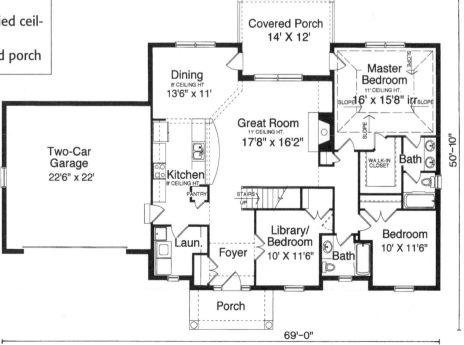

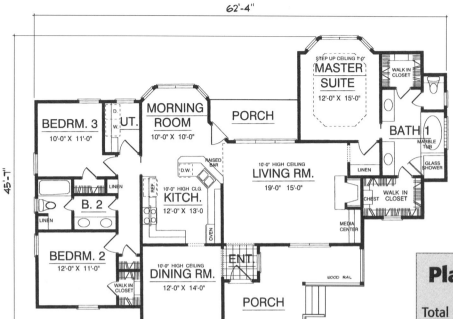

62'-4"

45'-7"

BEDRM. 3
10'-0" X 11'-0"

D.W.

UT.

MORNING ROOM
10"-0" X 10'-0"

PORCH

STEP UP CEILING 1'-0"
MASTER SUITE
12'-0" X 15'-0"

WALK IN CLOSET

BATH 1

MARBLE TUB

GLASS SHOWER

LINEN

B. 2

LINEN

RAISED BAR

D.W.

10'-0" HIGH CLG.
KITCH.
12'-0" X 13'-0

REF.

10'-0" HIGH CEILING
LIVING RM.
19'-0" 15'-0"

LINEN

CHEST

WALK IN CLOSET

MEDIA CENTER

BEDRM. 2
12'-0" X 11'-0"

WALK IN CLOSET

OVEN

10'-0" HIGH CEILING
DINING RM.
12'-0" X 14'-0"

ENT.

WOOD RAIL

PORCH

WOOD RAIL

Plan #532-030D-0003
Price Code B

Total Living Area: 1,753 Sq. Ft.

Home has 3 bedrooms, 2 baths and slab or crawl space foundation, please specify when ordering.

Special features
- Large front porch has charming appeal
- Kitchen with breakfast bar overlooks morning room and accesses covered porch
- Master suite has amenities such as a private bath, spacious closets and sunny bay window

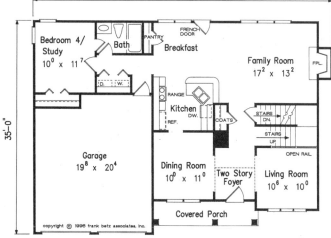

First Floor
1,103 sq. ft.

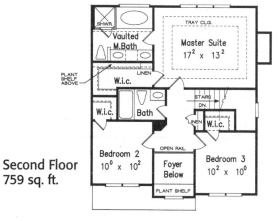

Second Floor
759 sq. ft.

Plan #532-035D-0038
Price Code C

Total Living Area: 1,862 Sq. Ft.

Home has 4 bedrooms, 3 baths, 2-car garage and walk-out basement or crawl space foundation, please specify when ordering.

Special features

- Dining and living rooms flank grand two-story foyer
- Open floor plan combines kitchen, breakfast and family rooms
- Study is tucked away on first floor for privacy
- Second floor bedrooms have walk-in closets

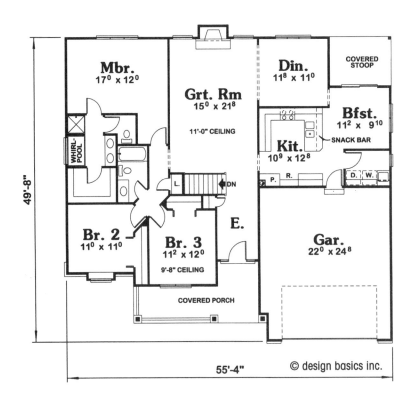

Mbr.
17⁰ x 12⁰

Grt. Rm
15⁰ x 21⁸

11'-0" CEILING

WHIRL-POOL

Br. 2
11⁰ x 11⁰

Br. 3
11² x 12⁰

9'-8" CEILING

E.

DN

L.

Din.
11⁸ x 11⁰

COVERED STOOP

Bfst.
11² x 9¹⁰

SNACK BAR

Kit.
10⁹ x 12⁸

P.   R.   D. W.

Gar.
22⁰ x 24⁸

COVERED PORCH

49'-8"

55'-4"

© design basics inc.

Plan #532-026D-0137
Price Code B

Total Living Area: 1,758 Sq. Ft.

Home has 3 bedrooms, 2 baths, 2-car garage and basement foundation.

Special features

- Secluded covered porch off break-fast area is a charming touch
- Great room and dining area combine for terrific entertaining possibilities
- Master bedroom has all the amenities
- Spacious foyer opens into a large great room with 11' ceiling

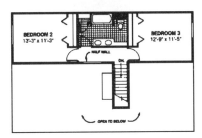

Second Floor
480 sq. ft.

BEDROOM 2
13'-3" x 11'-3"

BEDROOM 3
12'-9" x 11'-5"

HALF WALL

OPEN TO BELOW

Plan #532-008D-0056
Price Code B
Total Living Area: 1,704 Sq. Ft.

Home has 3 bedrooms, 2 1/2 baths, 2-car rear entry garage and basement foundation, drawings also include a slab foundation.

Special features
- Sensational large front porch for summer evenings and rear breeze-way for enjoying the outdoors
- Entry leads to dining/living area featuring a sloped ceiling and second floor balcony overlook
- Sophisticated master bedroom is complemented by a luxury bath with separate shower and toilet area
- Two good-sized bedrooms share a centrally located bath

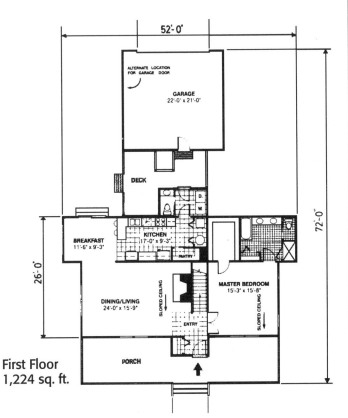

52'-0"

ALTERNATE LOCATION FOR GARAGE DOOR

GARAGE
22'-0" x 21'-0"

72'-0"

DECK

26'-0"

BREAKFAST
11'-6" x 9'-3"

KITCHEN
17'-0" x 9'-3"

PANTRY

SLOPED CEILING

DINING/LIVING
24'-0" x 15'-9"

MASTER BEDROOM
15'-3" x 15'-8"

SLOPED CEILING

ENTRY

PORCH

First Floor
1,224 sq. ft.

Plan #532-024D-0004
Price Code B
Total Living Area: 1,500 Sq. Ft.

Home has 3 bedrooms, 2 baths, 2-car garage and slab foundation.

Special features
- Living room features corner fireplace adding warmth
- Master bedroom has all the amenities including a walk-in closet, private bath and porch access
- Sunny bayed breakfast room is cheerful and bright

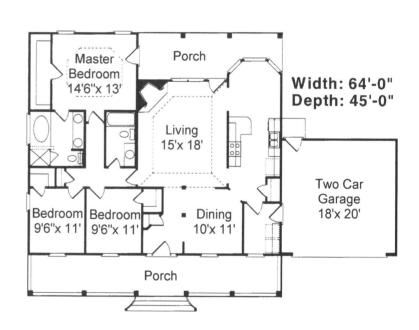

Width: 64'-0"
Depth: 45'-0"

Plan #532-039D-0012
Price Code C

Total Living Area: 1,815 Sq. Ft.

Home has 3 bedrooms, 2 1/2 baths, 2-car side entry garage and basement foundation.

Special features

- Second floor has built-in desk in hall which is ideal as a computer work station or mini office area
- Two doors into laundry area make it handy from master bedroom and the rest of the home
- Inviting covered porch
- Lots of counterspace and cabinetry in kitchen

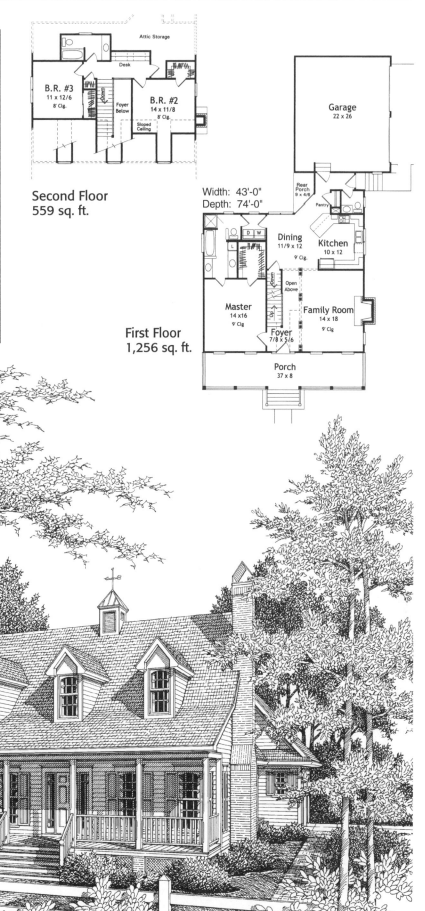

Second Floor
559 sq. ft.

Width: 43'-0"
Depth: 74'-0"

First Floor
1,256 sq. ft.

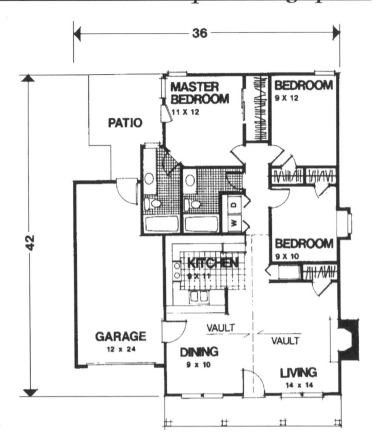

Plan #532-013D-0001
Price Code AA

Total Living Area: 1,050 Sq. Ft.

Home has 3 bedrooms, 2 baths, 1-car garage and basement or slab foundation, please specify when ordering.

Special features

- Master bedroom has its own private bath and access to the outdoors onto a private patio
- Vaulted ceilings in the living and dining areas create a feeling of spaciousness
- Laundry closet is convenient to all bedrooms
- Efficient U-shaped kitchen

Bay Creates Bright Sunroom

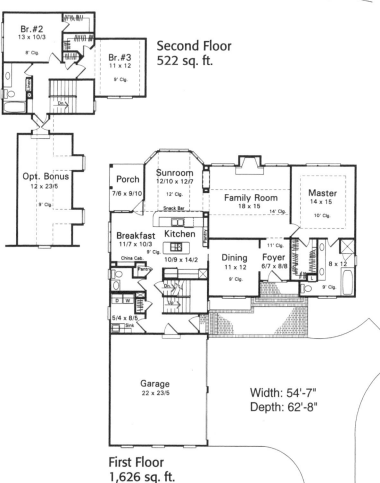

Br. #2
13 x 10/3

8' Clg.

Br. #3
11 x 12

9' Clg.

Second Floor
522 sq. ft.

Opt. Bonus
12 x 23/5

9' Clg.

Porch
7/6 x 9/10

Sunroom
12/10 x 12/7

12' Clg.

Snack Bar

Family Room
18 x 15

14' Clg.

Master
14 x 15

10' Clg.

Breakfast
11/7 x 10/3

Kitchen
10/9 x 14/2

9' Clg.

China Cab.

Pantry

Dining
11 x 12

9' Clg.

Foyer
6/7 x 8/8

11' Clg.

8 x 12

9' Clg.

D   W

5/4 x 8/5

Sink

Garage
22 x 23/5

Width: 54'-7"
Depth: 62'-8"

First Floor
1,626 sq. ft.

Plan #532-039D-0021
Price Code C
Total Living Area: 2,148 Sq. Ft.

Home has 3 bedrooms, 2 1/2 baths, 2-car side entry garage and basement foundation.

Special features
- Cheerful bayed sunroom has attached porch and overlooks kitchen and breakfast area
- Varied ceiling heights throughout the entire plan
- All bedrooms have walk-in closets
- Laundry area includes handy sink
- Optional bonus room on the second floor has an additional 336 square feet of living area

Plan #532-008D-0042
Price Code B
Total Living Area: 1,668 Sq. Ft.

Home has 3 bedrooms, 2 baths, 2-car garage and partial basement/crawl space foundation, drawings also include crawl space and slab foundations.

Special features
- Simple, but attractively styled ranch home is perfect for a narrow lot
- Front entry porch flows into foyer which connects to living room
- Garage entrance to home leads to kitchen through mud room/laundry area
- U-shaped kitchen opens to dining area and family room
- Three bedrooms are situated at the rear of the home with two full baths
- Master bedroom has walk-in closet

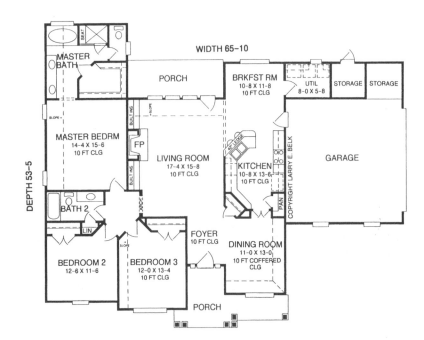

Plan #532-019D-0010
Price Code C

Total Living Area: 1,890 Sq. Ft.

Home has 3 bedrooms, 2 baths, 2-car side entry garage and crawl space foundation, drawings also include slab foundation.

Special features

- 10' ceilings give this home a spacious feel
- Efficient kitchen has breakfast bar which overlooks living room
- Master bedroom has a private bath with walk-in closet

Plan #532-024D-0009
Price Code B

Total Living Area: 1,704 Sq. Ft.

Home has 3 bedrooms, 2 baths and slab foundation.

Special features

■ Open floor plan combines foyer, dining and living rooms together for an open airy feeling

■ Kitchen has island that adds work-space and storage

■ Bedrooms are situated together and secluded from the rest of the home

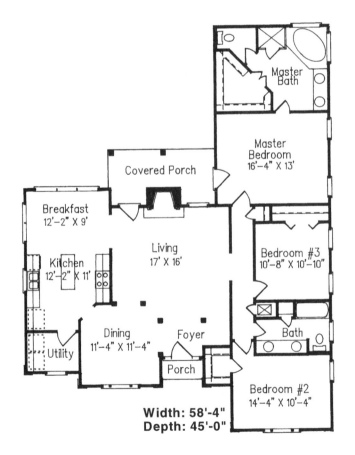

Width: 58'-4"
Depth: 45'-0"

Second Floor
520 sq. ft.

First Floor
973 sq. ft.

Width: 40'-0"
Depth: 41'-0"

Plan #532-034D-0013
Price Code A

Total Living Area: 1,493 Sq. Ft.

Home has 3 bedrooms, 2 1/2 baths, 2-car garage and basement foundation.

Special features

- First floor master bedroom maintains privacy
- Dining and great rooms have a feeling of spaciousness with two-story high ceilings
- Utilities are conveniently located near the garage entrance

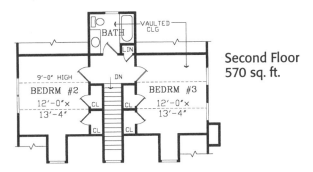

Second Floor
570 sq. ft.

BATH — VAULTED CLG

LIN

DN

9'-0" HIGH

BEDRM #2
12'-0" x
13'-4"

CL CL

BEDRM #3
12'-0" x
13'-4"

CL CL

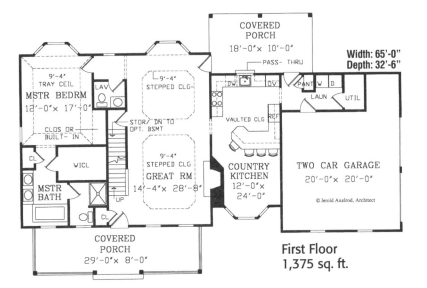

COVERED PORCH
18'-0" x 10'-0"

PASS-THRU

DW

DV

PANT W D

LAUN UTIL

9'-4" TRAY CEIL
MSTR BEDRM
12'-0" x 17'-0"

LAV

9'-4" STEPPED CLG

VAULTED CLG

REF

CLOS OR BUILT-IN

STOR/ DN TO OPT. BSMT

CL

WICL

9'-4" STEPPED CLG
GREAT RM
14'-4" x 28'-8"

UP

MSTR BATH

CL

COUNTRY KITCHEN
12'-0" x 24'-0"

TWO CAR GARAGE
20'-0" x 20'-0"

© Jerold Axelrod, Architect

COVERED PORCH
29'-0" x 8'-0"

First Floor
1,375 sq. ft.

Width: 65'-0"
Depth: 32'-6"

Plan #532-016D-0051
Price Code D
Total Living Area: 1,945 Sq. Ft.

Home has 3 bedrooms, 2 1/2 baths, 2-car side entry garage and basement, crawl space or slab foundation, please specify when ordering.

Special features
- Great room has a stepped ceiling and a fireplace
- Bayed dining area with stepped ceiling and French door leading to a covered porch
- Master bedroom has a tray ceiling, a bay window and a large walk-in closet

TO ORDER BLUEPRINTS USE THE FORM ON PAGE 288 OR CALL TOLL-FREE **1-800-DREAM HOME** (373-2646)

Second Floor
570 sq. ft.

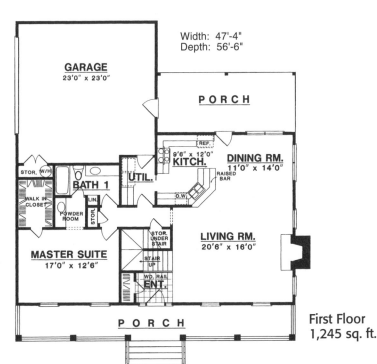

Width: 47'-4"
Depth: 56'-6"

First Floor
1,245 sq. ft.

Plan #532-030D-0005
Price Code C

Total Living Area: 1,815 Sq. Ft.

Home has 3 bedrooms, 2 baths, 2-car side entry garage and basement, crawl space or slab foundation, please specify when ordering.

Special features
- Well-designed kitchen opens to dining room and features raised breakfast bar
- First floor master suite has walk-in closet
- Front and back porches unite this home with the outdoors

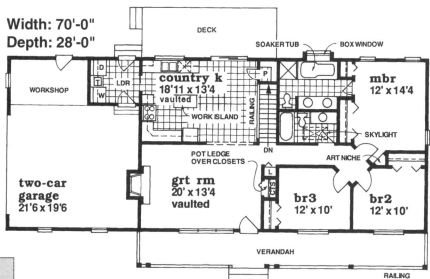

Width: 70'-0"
Depth: 28'-0"

DECK

SOAKER TUB

BOX WINDOW

WORKSHOP

LDR

country k
18'11 x 13'4
vaulted

WORK ISLAND

RAILING

P

mbr
12' x 14'4

SKYLIGHT

POT LEDGE
OVER CLOSETS

DN

ART NICHE

two-car garage
21'6 x 19'6

grt rm
20' x 13'4
vaulted

br3
12' x 10'

br2
12' x 10'

VERANDAH

RAILING

Plan #532-062D-0050
Price Code A

Total Living Area: 1,408 Sq. Ft.

Home has 3 bedrooms, 2 baths, 2-car side entry garage and basement or crawl space foundation, please specify when ordering.

Special features

- A bright country kitchen boasts an abundance of counterspace and cupboards

- The front entry is sheltered by a broad verandah

- A spa tub is brightened by a box-bay window in the master bath

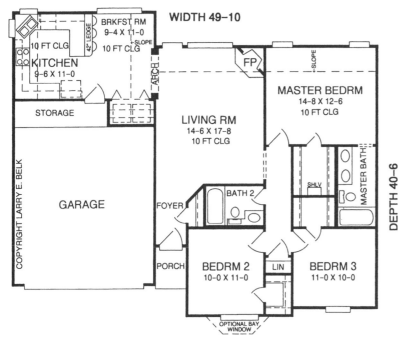

WIDTH 49–10

BRKFST RM
9-4 X 11-0

SLOPE

10 FT CLG

42" LEDGE

10 FT CLG

KITCHEN
9-6 X 11-0

STORAGE

ARCH

FP

SLOPE

MASTER BEDRM
14-8 X 12-6
10 FT CLG

LIVING RM
14-6 X 17-8
10 FT CLG

COPYRIGHT LARRY E. BELK

GARAGE

FOYER

BATH 2

SHLV

MASTER BATH

DEPTH 40-6

PORCH

BEDRM 2
10-0 X 11-0

LIN

BEDRM 3
11-0 X 10-0

OPTIONAL BAY
WINDOW

Plan #532-019D-0003
Price Code A

Total Living Area: 1,310 Sq. Ft.

Home has 3 bedrooms, 2 baths, 2-car garage and crawl space foundation, drawings also include slab foundation.

Special features

- Family room features a corner fireplace adding warmth
- Efficiently designed kitchen has a corner sink with windows
- Master bedroom includes a large walk-in closet and private bath

Second Floor
630 sq. ft.

Plan #532-008D-0088
Price Code C
Total Living Area: 1,850 Sq. Ft.

Home has 3 bedrooms, 2 1/2 baths, 2-car garage and basement foundation.

Special features
■ Large living room with fireplace is illuminated by three second story skylights

■ Living and dining rooms are separated by a low wall while the dining room and kitchen are separated by a snack bar creating a spacious atmosphere

■ Master bedroom has a huge bath with double vanity and large walk-in closet

■ Two second floor bedrooms share a uniquely designed bath with skylight

First Floor
1,220 sq. ft.

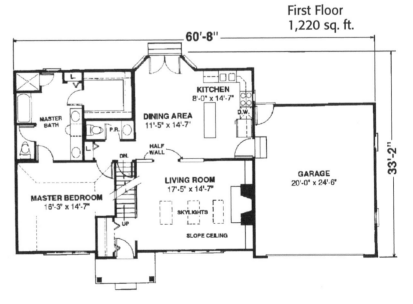

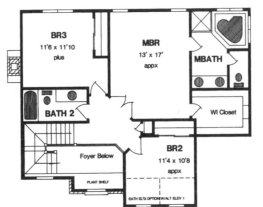

BR3
11'6 x 11'10
plus

MBR
13' x 17'
appx

MBATH

BATH 2

WI Closet

Second Floor
942 sq. ft.

Foyer Below

BR2
11'4 x 10'8
appx

PLANT SHELF

CATH CL'G OPTION W/ALT ELEV 1

Plan #532-034D-0016
Price Code C

Total Living Area: 1,873 Sq. Ft.

Home has 3 bedrooms, 2 1/2 baths,
2-car garage and basement foundation.

Special features

- Formal dining area in the front of the house is conveniently located near kitchen

- Large great room has fireplace and lots of windows

- Master bedroom has double-door entry with a private bath

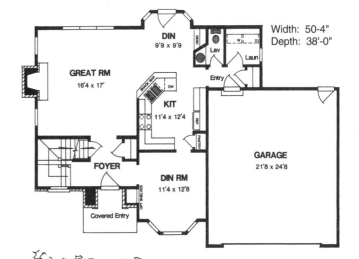

DIN
9'9 x 9'9

Lav

Laun

Entry

GREAT RM
16'4 x 17'

KIT
11'4 x 12'4

DW

REF

PANTRY

GARAGE
21'8 x 24'8

Width: 50-4"
Depth: 38'-0"

FOYER

DIN RM
11'4 x 12'8

OPT SHELVES

Covered Entry

First Floor
931 sq. ft.

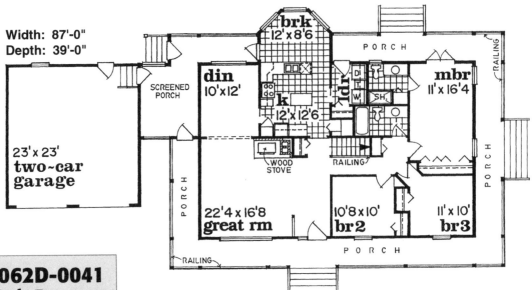

Width: 87'-0"
Depth: 39'-0"

SCREENED PORCH

23' x 23'
two~car garage

brk
12' x 8'6

PORCH

din
10' x 12'

mbr
11' x 16'4

RAILING

k
12' x 12'6

WOOD STOVE

RAILING

PORCH

PORCH

great rm
22'4 x 16'8

br 2
10'8 x 10'

br 3
11' x 10'

RAILING

PORCH

Plan #532-062D-0041
Price Code B

Total Living Area:	1,541 Sq. Ft.

Home has 3 bedrooms, 2 baths, 2-car garage and basement or crawl space foundation, please specify when ordering.

Special features

- Dining area offers access to a screened porch for outdoor dining and entertaining
- Country kitchen features a center island and a breakfast bay for casual meals
- Great room is warmed by a wood-stove

Second Floor
543 sq. ft.

Attic

Family Room Below

Bath

Bedroom 4
12⁸ x 12⁰

W.i.c.

LINEN

OPEN RAIL

STAIRS DN.

OVERLOOK

W.i.c.

OPEN RAIL

Foyer Below

Bedroom 3
11⁰ x 10⁸

W.i.c.

Opt. Bonus Room
11⁵ x 19²

VAULT

Plan #532-035D-0040
Price Code C

Total Living Area: 2,126 Sq. Ft.

Home has 4 bedrooms, 3 baths, 2-car side entry garage and walk-out basement, crawl space or slab foundation, please specify when ordering.

Special features
- ■ Kitchen overlooks vaulted family room with a handy serving bar
- ■ Two-story foyer creates an airy feeling
- ■ Second floor includes an optional bonus room with an additional 251 square feet of living area

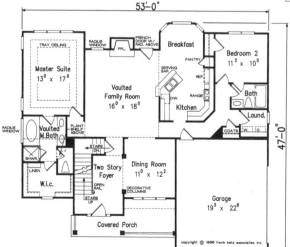

53'-0"

47'-0"

TRAY CEILING

Master Suite
13⁰ x 17⁰

RADIUS WINDOW

FPL

FRENCH DOOR W/ RAD. ABOVE

Breakfast

PANTRY

Bedroom 2
11² x 10⁰

SERVING BAR

REF.

RANGE

Vaulted Family Room
16⁰ x 18⁰

D.W.

Kitchen

Bath

Laund.

RADIUS WINDOW

Vaulted M.Bath

PLANT SHELF ABOVE

COATS

W.

D.

SHWR.

STAIRS DN.

Two Story Foyer

Dining Room
11⁰ x 12²

LINEN

OPEN RAIL

W.i.c.

STAIRS UP

DECORATIVE COLUMNS

Garage
19⁵ x 22⁸

Covered Porch

copyright © 1996 frank betz associates, inc.

First Floor
1,583 sq. ft.

Width: 62'-4"
Depth: 51'-0"

Plan #532-047D-0036
Price Code C
Total Living Area: 2,140 Sq. Ft.

Home has 4 bedrooms, 3 baths, 2-car side entry garage and slab foundation.

Special features
- Living and dining areas are traditionally separated by foyer
- Media wall and fireplace are located in cozy family room
- Generous master bedroom has sliding glass doors onto patio, walk-in closet and a private bath

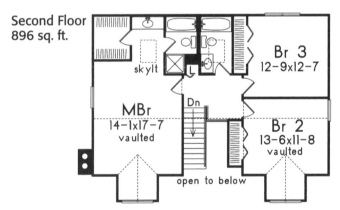

Second Floor
896 sq. ft.

skylt

Br 3
12-9x12-7

MBr
14-1x17-7
vaulted

Dn

Br 2
13-6x11-8
vaulted

open to below

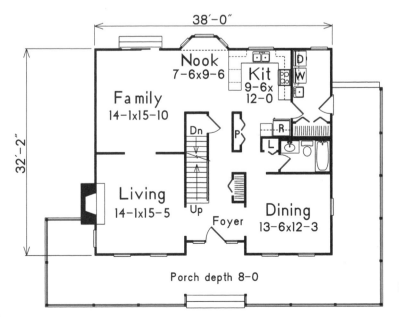

38′-0″

32′-2″

Nook
7-6x9-6

Kit
9-6x
12-0

Family
14-1x15-10

Dn

P

R

L

Living
14-1x15-5

Up

Foyer

Dining
13-6x12-3

Porch depth 8-0

First Floor
1,216 sq. ft.

Plan #532-008D-0085
Price Code C

Total Living Area: 2,112 Sq. Ft.

Home has 3 bedrooms, 2 1/2 baths and basement foundation, drawings also include crawl space foundation.

Special features
- Kitchen efficiently connects to the formal dining area
- Nook located between family room and kitchen makes an ideal breakfast area
- Both baths on second floor feature skylights

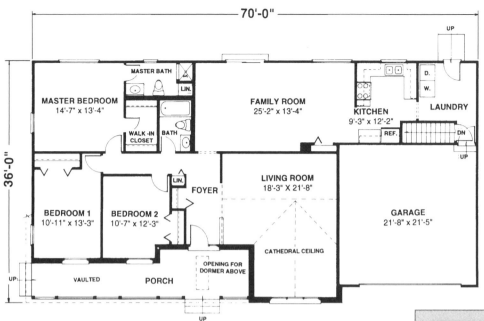

70'-0"

36'-0"

MASTER BATH

MASTER BEDROOM
14'-7" x 13'-4"

LIN.

WALK-IN CLOSET

BATH

FAMILY ROOM
25'-2" x 13'-4"

KITCHEN
9'-3" x 12'-2"

D.

W.

LAUNDRY

REF.

DN

UP

UP

LIN.

FOYER

LIVING ROOM
18'-3" X 21'-8"

GARAGE
21'-8" x 21'-5"

BEDROOM 1
10'-11" x 13'-3"

BEDROOM 2
10'-7" x 12'-3"

CATHEDRAL CEILING

UP

VAULTED

PORCH

OPENING FOR DORMER ABOVE

UP

Plan #532-008D-0101
Price Code C

Total Living Area: 1,820 Sq. Ft.

Home has 3 bedrooms, 2 baths, 2-car garage and basement foundation.

Special features
- Living room has a stunning cathedral ceiling
- Spacious laundry room with easy access to kitchen, garage and the outdoors
- Plenty of closet space throughout
- Covered front porch enhances outdoor living

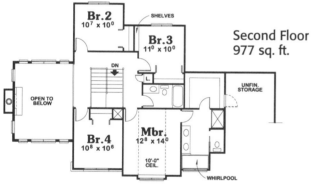

Second Floor
977 sq. ft.

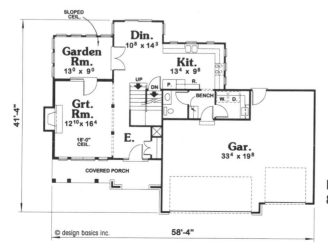

First Floor
837 sq. ft.

Plan #532-026D-0141
Price Code C

Total Living Area: 1,814 Sq. Ft.

Home has 4 bedrooms, 2 1/2 baths, 3-car garage and basement foundation.

Special features
- Handy bench located outside laundry area for changing
- Charming garden room located off great room brings in the outdoors
- Kitchen features lots of cabinetry and counterspace

Plan #532-065D-0028
Price Code B

Total Living Area: 1,611 Sq. Ft.

Home has 3 bedrooms, 2 baths, 2-car side entry garage and basement foundation.

Special features

■ Sliding doors lead to a delightful screened porch creating a wonderful summer retreat

■ Master bedroom has a lavishly appointed dressing room and large walk-in closet

■ The kitchen offers an abundance of cabinets and counterspace with convenient access to the laundry room and garage

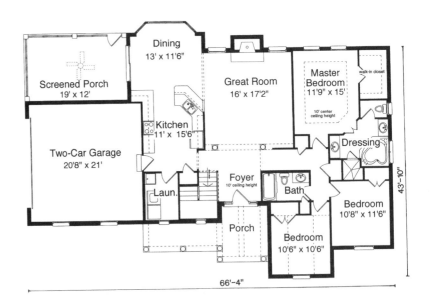

Plan #532-026D-0142
Price Code C

Total Living Area: 2,188 Sq. Ft.

Home has 3 bedrooms, 2 baths, 3-car side entry garage and basement foundation.

Special features

- Master bedroom includes a private covered porch, sitting area and two large walk-in closets
- Spacious kitchen has center island, snack bar and laundry access
- Great room has a 10' ceiling and a dramatic corner fireplace

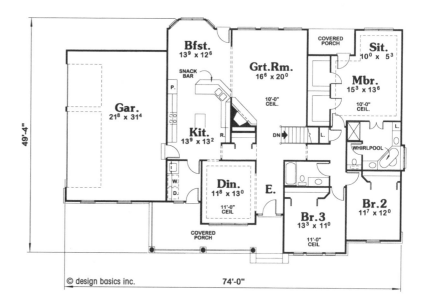

© design basics inc.

Our Blueprint Packages Offer...

Quality plans for building your future, with extras that provide unsurpassed value, ensure good construction and long-term enjoyment.

A quality home - one that looks good, functions well, and provides years of enjoyment - is a product of many things - design, materials, craftsmanship. But it's also the result of outstanding blueprints - the actual plans and specifications that tell the builder exactly how to build your home.

And with our BLUEPRINT PACKAGES you get the absolute best. A complete set of blueprints is available for every design in this book. These "working drawings," are highly detailed, resulting in two key benefits:

- *Better understanding by the contractor of how to build your home, and...*
- *More accurate construction estimates.*

When you purchase one of our designs, you'll receive all of the BLUEPRINT components shown here - elevations, foundation plan, floor plans, sections, and/or details. Other helpful building aids are also available to help make your dream home a reality.

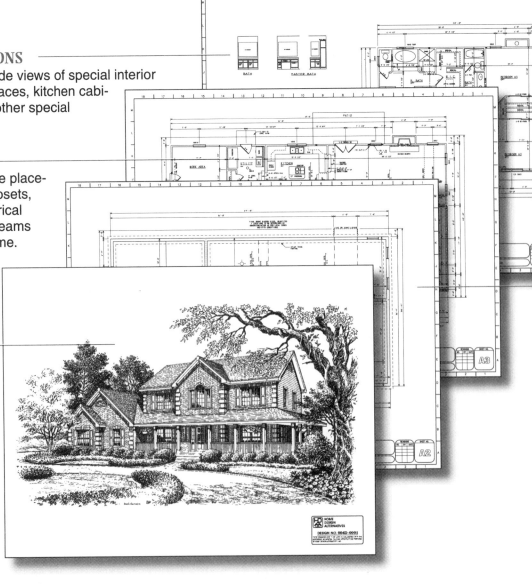

INTERIOR ELEVATIONS
Interior elevations provide views of special interior elements such as fireplaces, kitchen cabinets, built-in units and other special features of the home.

FLOOR PLANS
The floor plans show the placement of walls, doors, closets, plumbing fixtures, electrical outlets, columns, and beams for each level of the home.

COVER SHEET
The cover sheet is the artist's rendering of the exterior of the home. It will give you an idea of how your home will look when completed and landscaped.

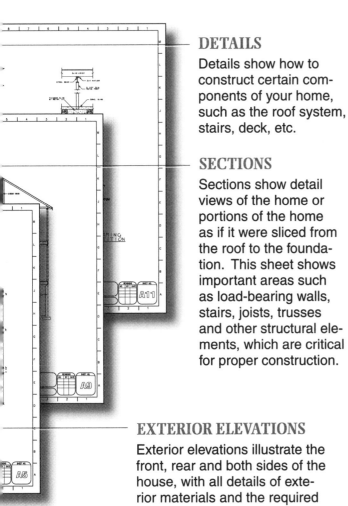

DETAILS

Details show how to construct certain components of your home, such as the roof system, stairs, deck, etc.

SECTIONS

Sections show detail views of the home or portions of the home as if it were sliced from the roof to the foundation. This sheet shows important areas such as load-bearing walls, stairs, joists, trusses and other structural elements, which are critical for proper construction.

EXTERIOR ELEVATIONS

Exterior elevations illustrate the front, rear and both sides of the house, with all details of exterior materials and the required dimensions.

FOUNDATION PLAN

The foundation plan shows the layout of the basement, crawl space, slab, or pier foundation. All necessary notations and dimensions are included. See plan page for the foundation types included. If the home plan you choose does not have your desired foundation type, our Customer Service Representatives can advise you on how to customize your foundation to suit your specific needs or site conditions.

Other Helpful Building Aids...

Your Blueprint Package contains the necessary construction information to build your home. We also offer the following products and services to save you time and money in the building process.

Express Delivery

Most orders are processed within 24 hours of receipt. Please allow 7-10 business days for delivery. If you need to place a rush order, please call us by 11:00 a.m. Monday-Friday CST and ask for express service (allow 1-2 business days).

Technical Assistance

If you have questions, call our technical support line at 1-314-770-2228 between 8:00 a.m. and 5:00 p.m. Monday-Friday CST. Whether it involves design modifications or field assistance, our designers are extremely familiar with all of our designs and will be happy to help you. We want your home to be everything you expect it to be.

Material List

Material lists are available for many of the plans in this publication. Each list gives you the quantity, dimensions and description of the building materials necessary to construct your home. You'll get faster and more accurate bids from your contractor while saving money by paying for only the materials you need. See the Home Plans Index on pages 286-287 for availability. **Cost: $125**

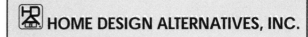 **HOME DESIGN ALTERNATIVES, INC.**

HOME PLANS INDEX

Shaded Plans Denote Lowe's Signature Series Plans

Plan Number	Sq. Ft.	Price Code	Page	Mat. List	Right Read. Reverse	Can. Ship.
532-001D-0013	1,882	D	80	•		
532-001D-0024	1,360	A	46	•		
532-001D-0025	1,998	D	84	•		
532-001D-0031	1,501	B	77	•		
532-001D-0035	1,396	A	81	•		
532-001D-0040	864	AAA	25	•		
532-001D-0041	1,000	AA	45	•		
532-001D-0043	1,104	AA	49	•		
532-001D-0045	1,197	AA	59	•		
532-001D-0048	1,400	A	19	•		
532-001D-0050	1,827	C	34	•		
532-001D-0053	1,344	A	32	•		
532-001D-0056	1,705	B	90	•		
532-001D-0058	1,720	B	86	•		
532-001D-0059	2,050	C	104	•		
532-001D-0061	1,875	C	33	•		
532-001D-0064	2,262	D	28	•		
532-001D-0067	1,285	B	61	•		
532-001D-0071	1,440	A	47	•		
532-001D-0072	1,288	A	31	•		
532-001D-0074	1,664	B	57	•		
532-001D-0081	1,160	AA	67	•		
532-001D-0086	1,154	AA	22	•		
532-001D-0087	1,230	A	72	•		
532-001D-0093	1,120	AA	17	•		
532-003D-0001	2,058	C	60	•		
532-003D-0002	1,676	B	35	•		
532-003D-0005	1,708	B	9	•		
532-005D-0001	1,400	B	50	•		
532-006D-0003	1,674	B	53	•		
532-007D-0003	2,806	E	122	•		
532-007D-0010	1,721	C	23	•		
532-007D-0014	1,985	C	63	•		
532-007D-0017	1,882	C	10	•		
532-007D-0018	1,941	C	110	•		
532-007D-0030	1,140	AA	16	•		
532-007D-0031	1,092	AA	109	•		
532-007D-0035	1,619	B	85	•		
532-007D-0037	1,403	A	5	•		
532-007D-0038	1,524	B	18	•		
532-007D-0045	1,321	A	103	•		
532-007D-0049	1,791	C	37	•		
532-007D-0050	2,723	E	52	•		
532-007D-0054	1,575	B	39	•		
532-007D-0055	2,029	D	13	•		
532-007D-0060	1,268	B	78	•		
532-007D-0061	1,340	A	89	•		
532-007D-0067	1,761	B	126	•		
532-007D-0068	1,384	B	36	•		
532-007D-0085	1,787	B	102	•		
532-007D-0102	1,452	A	48	•		
532-007D-0103	1,231	A	24	•		
532-007D-0104	969	AA	107	•		
532-007D-0105	1,084	AA	62	•		
532-007D-0106	1,200	A	112	•		
532-007D-0110	1,169	AA	51	•		
532-008D-0004	1,643	B	41	•		
532-008D-0010	1,440	A	106	•		
532-008D-0045	1,540	B	96	•		
532-010D-0006	1,170	AA	76	•		
532-014D-0015	1,941	C	55	•		
532-017D-0005	1,367	B	75	•		
532-017D-0007	1,567	C	79	•		
532-018D-0006	1,742	B	54	•		
532-018D-0008	2,109	C	27	•		
532-021D-0006	1,600	C	14	•		
532-021D-0007	1,868	D	101	•		
532-021D-0011	1,800	D	12	•		
532-021D-0012	1,672	C	99	•		
532-021D-0016	1,600	B	56	•		
532-022D-0002	1,246	A	26	•		
532-022D-0014	1,556	B	66	•		
532-023D-0016	1,609	B	70	•		
532-023D-0018	1,556	B	83	•		
532-029D-0002	1,619	B	91	•		
532-033D-0012	1,546	C	40	•		
532-037D-0002	1,816	C	95	•		
532-037D-0003	1,996	D	111	•		
532-037D-0006	1,772	C	38	•		
532-037D-0009	2,059	C	71	•		
532-037D-0016	2,066	C	42	•		
532-037D-0020	1,994	D	11	•		
532-040D-0001	1,814	D	30	•		
532-040D-0003	1,475	B	15	•		
532-040D-0007	2,073	D	6	•		
532-040D-0015	1,655	B	88	•		
532-040D-0026	1,393	B	82	•		
532-040D-0027	1,597	C	98	•		
532-041D-0001	2,003	D	58	•		
532-041D-0004	1,195	AA	69	•		
532-041D-0006	1,189	AA	44	•		
532-045D-0017	954	AA	20	•		
532-048D-0001	1,865	D	105	•		
532-048D-0011	1,550	B	29	•		
532-053D-0002	1,668	C	7	•		
532-053D-0029	1,220	A	93	•		
532-053D-0030	1,657	B	8	•		
532-053D-0032	1,404	A	73	•		
532-053D-0041	1,364	A	21	•		
532-053D-0058	1,818	C	65	•		
532-058D-0002	2,059	C	74	•		
532-058D-0006	1,339	A	97	•		
532-058D-0012	1,143	AA	92	•		
532-058D-0013	1,073	AA	68	•		
532-058D-0016	1,558	B	87	•		
532-058D-0020	1,428	A	64	•		
532-058D-0021	1,477	A	100	•		
532-058D-0025	2,164	C	121	•		
532-058D-0026	1,819	C	127	•		
532-058D-0029	1,000	AA	116	•		
532-058D-0030	990	AA	117	•		
532-058D-0033	1,440	A	43	•		
532-058D-0037	2,179	C	115	•		
532-058D-0038	1,680	B	120	•		
532-058D-0039	2,240	D	125	•		
532-058D-0043	1,277	A	118	•		
532-058D-0046	2,547	D	124	•		
532-068D-0003	1,784	B	108	•		
532-068D-0004	1,969	C	94	•		
532-068D-0005	1,433	A	114	•		
532-068D-0006	1,399	A	113	•		
532-068D-0007	1,599	B	123	•		
532-068D-0009	2,128	C	128	•		
532-068D-0010	1,849	C	119	•		
532-008D-0001	2,137	C	137	•		
532-008D-0008	2,137	C	155	•		
532-008D-0011	1,550	B	180	•		
532-008D-0012	1,232	A	169	•		
532-008D-0013	1,345	A	203	•		
532-008D-0026	1,120	AA	205	•		
532-008D-0042	1,668	B	266	•		
532-008D-0054	1,574	B	132	•		
532-008D-0056	1,704	B	261	•		
532-008D-0063	2,086	C	242	•		
532-008D-0072	1,200	A	256	•		
532-008D-0076	1,922	C	221	•		
532-008D-0084	1,704	B	231	•		
532-008D-0085	2,112	C	279	•		
532-008D-0088	1,850	C	274	•		
532-008D-0089	1,907	C	156	•		
532-008D-0090	1,364	A	194	•		
532-008D-0094	1,364	A	189	•		
532-008D-0097	1,948	C	215	•		
532-008D-0101	1,820	C	280	•		
532-008D-0103	1,128	AA	207	•		
532-008D-0104	1,400	A	200	•		
532-008D-0122	1,364	A	151	•		
532-008D-0143	1,299	A	185	•		
532-008D-0145	1,750	B	196	•		
532-008D-0168	1,092	AA	217	•		
532-008D-0178	1,872	C	175	•		
532-008D-0179	1,973	C	244	•		
532-011D-0001	1,275	C	179			•
532-011D-0005	1,467	C	211	•	•	•
532-011D-0011	2,155	C	190	•		
532-011D-0021	1,464	C	233	•		
532-011D-0022	1,994	D	161	•		
532-013D-0001	1,050	AA	264	•		
532-013D-0011	1,643	B	157	•		
532-013D-0015	1,787	B	143	•		
532-013D-0022	1,992	C	225	•	•	•
532-013D-0025	2,097	C	152	•		
532-016D-0001	1,783	D	229	•		
532-016D-0049	1,793	B	197	•		
532-016D-0051	1,945	D	270	•		
532-016D-0055	1,040	B	147	•		
532-016D-0062	1,380	A	150	•		
532-019D-0002	1,282	A	163	•		
532-019D-0003	1,310	A	273	•		
532-019D-0009	1,862	C	144	•		
532-019D-0010	1,890	C	267	•		
532-019D-0011	1,955	C	228	•		
532-019D-0013	1,932	C	241	•		
532-020D-0002	1,434	A	195	•		
532-020D-0003	1,420	A	182	•		
532-020D-0005	1,770	B	212	•		
532-020D-0007	1,828	C	177	•		
532-020D-0009	2,123	E	192	•		
532-020D-0010	2,194	C	209	•		
532-020D-0014	1,150	AA	181	•		
532-020D-0015	1,191	AA	178	•		
532-024D-0002	1,405	A	210	•		
532-024D-0004	1,500	B	262	•		
532-024D-0007	1,609	B	238	•		
532-024D-0009	1,704	B	268	•		
532-024D-0010	1,737	B	131	•		
532-025D-0002	1,397	A	176	•		
532-025D-0005	1,429	A	251	•		
532-025D-0010	1,677	B	249	•		
532-025D-0012	1,634	B	199	•		
532-025D-0013	1,686	B	191	•		
532-026D-0110	1,999	C	202	•		
532-026D-0112	1,911	C	138	•	•	•
532-026D-0122	1,850	C	198	•	•	•
532-026D-0123	1,998	C	206	•		
532-026D-0130	1,479	A	170	•		
532-026D-0137	1,758	B	260	•	•	•
532-026D-0141	1,814	C	281	•	•	•
532-026D-0142	2,188	C	283	•		
532-026D-0154	1,392	A	208	•		
532-026D-0155	1,691	B	135	•		
532-028D-0003	1,716	B	188			•
532-028D-0004	1,785	B	218			•
532-028D-0006	1,700	B	159	•		

Plan Number	Sq. Ft.	Price Code	Page	Mat. List	Right Read. Reverse	Can. Ship.	Plan Number	Sq. Ft.	Price Code	Page	Mat. List	Right Read. Reverse	Can. Ship.
532-028D-0008	2,156	C	234		•		532-043D-0003	1,890	C	223			
532-028D-0017	2,669	E	160		•		532-043D-0005	1,734	B	214			
532-030D-0001	1,374	A	236				532-043D-0009	1,751	B	220			
532-030D-0002	1,429	A	254				532-047D-0020	1,783	B	183			
532-030D-0003	1,753	B	258				532-047D-0036	2,140	C	278	•		
532-030D-0004	1,791	B	162				532-049D-0006	1,771	B	166	•		
532-030D-0005	1,815	C	271				532-049D-0008	1,937	C	201	•		
532-030D-0006	1,896	C	232				532-049D-0010	1,669	B	171			
532-034D-0013	1,493	A	269				532-049D-0012	1,295	A	224	•		
532-034D-0014	1,792	B	129				532-052D-0005	1,268	A	141			
532-034D-0015	1,868	C	213				532-052D-0011	1,325	A	230	•		
532-034D-0016	1,873	C	275				532-052D-0013	1,379	A	154			
532-034D-0019	1,992	C	193				532-052D-0028	1,683	B	186			
532-034D-0020	2,018	C	227				532-052D-0036	1,772	B	222			
532-034D-0022	2,097	C	165				532-052D-0061	2,036	C	255			
532-035D-0003	2,115	C	250	•			532-055D-0017	1,525	B	136	•	•	•
532-035D-0011	1,945	C	148	•			532-055D-0022	2,107	C	237	•	•	•
532-035D-0021	1,978	C	133	•			532-055D-0030	2,107	C	164	•	•	•
532-035D-0028	1,779	B	248	•			532-055D-0044	1,797	B	145	•	•	•
532-035D-0031	2,052	C	245	•			532-055D-0051	1,848	C	247	•	•	•
532-035D-0032	1,856	C	219	•			532-056D-0009	1,606	B	130			
532-035D-0036	2,193	C	167	•			532-056D-0022	1,817	C	168			
532-035D-0038	1,862	C	259	•			532-056D-0024	1,093	AA	204			
532-035D-0039	2,201	D	153	•			532-062D-0041	1,541	B	276	•	•	•
532-035D-0040	2,126	C	277	•			532-062D-0048	1,543	B	239	•		•
532-035D-0047	1,818	C	252	•			532-062D-0050	1,408	A	272	•	•	•
532-035D-0048	1,915	C	226	•			532-062D-0052	1,795	B	149	•	•	•
532-036D-0048	1,830	C	158				532-062D-0055	1,583	B	187	•		•
532-036D-0056	1,604	B	246				532-065D-0017	1,856	C	253			
532-036D-0060	1,760	B	235				532-065D-0028	1,611	B	282			
532-039D-0001	1,253	A	174	•			532-065D-0032	1,544	B	139			
532-039D-0004	1,406	A	173	•			532-065D-0033	1,648	B	257			
532-039D-0012	1,815	C	263	•			532-065D-0034	1,509	B	243			
532-039D-0014	1,849	C	240	•			532-072D-0001	1,724	B	134			
532-039D-0015	1,855	C	184	•			532-072D-0002	1,551	A	146			
532-039D-0018	2,008	C	142	•			532-072D-0003	1,317	A	172			
532-039D-0019	2,009	C	216	•			532-072D-0004	1,926	C	140			
532-039D-0021	2,148	C	265	•									

OTHER GREAT PRODUCTS TO HELP YOU BUILD YOUR DREAM HOME

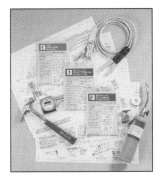

FRAMING, PLUMBING AND ELECTRICAL PLAN PACKAGES

Three separate packages offer homebuilders details for constructing various foundations; numerous floor, wall and roof framing techniques; simple to complex residential wiring; sump and water softener hookups; plumbing connection methods; installation of septic systems, and more. Each package includes three-dimensional illustrations and a glossary of terms. Purchase one or all three. **Cost: $20.00 each or all three for $40.00**
Note: These drawings do not pertain to a specific home plan.

THE LEGAL KIT

Avoid many legal pitfalls and build your home with confidence using the forms and contracts featured in this kit. Included are request for proposal documents, various fixed price and cost plus contracts, instructions on how and when to use each form, warranty statements and more. Save time and money before you break ground on your new home or start a remodeling project. All forms are reproducible. The kit is ideal for homebuilders and contractors. **Cost: $35.00**

Now that you've found the home plan you've been looking for, here are some suggestions on how to make your Dream Home a reality. To get started, order the type of plans that fit your particular situation.

Your Choices:

The 1-Set Study package - We offer a 1-set plan package so you can study your home in detail. This one set is considered a study set and is marked "not for construction." It is a copyright violation to reproduce blueprints.

The Minimum 5-Set package - If you're ready to start the construction process, this 5-set package is the minimum number of blueprint sets you will need. It will require keeping close track of each set so they can be used by multiple subcontractors and tradespeople.

The Standard 8-set package - For best results in terms of cost, schedule and quality of construction, we recommend you order eight (or more) sets of blueprints. Besides one set for yourself, additional sets of blueprints will be required by your mortgage lender, local building department, general contractor and all subcontractors working on foundation, electrical, plumbing, heating/air conditioning, carpentry work, etc.

Reproducible Masters - If you wish to make some minor design changes, you'll want to order reproducible masters. These drawings contain the same information as the blueprints but are printed on erasable and reproducible paper which clearly indicates your right to copy or reproduce. This will allow your builder or a local design professional to make the necessary drawing changes without the major expense of redrawing the plans. This package also allows you to print copies of the modified plans as needed. The right of building only one structure from these plans is licensed exclusively to the buyer. You may not use this design to build a second or multiple dwelling(s) without purchasing another blueprint. Each violation of the Copyright Law is punishable in a fine.

Mirror Reverse Sets - Plans can be printed in mirror reverse. These plans are useful when the house would fit your site better if all the rooms were on the opposite side than shown. They are simply a mirror image of the original drawings causing the lettering and dimensions to read backwards. Therefore, when ordering mirror reverse drawings, you must purchase at least one set of right-reading plans. Some of our plans are offered mirror reverse right-reading. This means the plan, lettering and dimensions are flipped but read correctly. See the Home Plans Index for availability.

How To Order

For fastest service, Call Toll-Free
1-800-DREAM HOME
(1-800-373-2646) 24 HOURS A DAY

Three Easy Ways To Order

1. CALL toll-free 1-877-373-2646 for credit card orders. Lowe's, MasterCard, Visa, Discover and American Express are accepted.

2. FAX your order to 1-314-770-2226.

3. MAIL the Order Form to:

   HDA, Inc.
   944 Anglum Road
   St. Louis, MO 63042

Order Form

Please send me -

PLAN NUMBER   532 - _____

PRICE CODE _____ *(see pages 286-287)*

Specify Foundation Type *(see plan page for availability)*
- ☐ Slab   ☐ Crawl space   ☐ Pier
- ☐ Basement   ☐ Walk-out basement
- ☐ Reproducible Masters $ _____
- ☐ Eight-Set Plan Package $ _____
- ☐ Five-Set Plan Package $ _____
- ☐ One-Set Study Package *(no mirror reverse)* $ _____
- ☐ Additional Plan Sets*
  - _____ (Qty.) at $45.00 each $ _____

Mirror Reverse*
- ☐ Right-reading $150 one-time charge
  - *(see index on pages 286-287 for availability)* $ _____
- ☐ Print in Mirror Reverse *(where right-reading is not available)*
  - _____ (Qty.) at $15.00 each $ _____
- ☐ Material List* $125 *(see pages 286-287)* $ _____
- ☐ Legal Kit *(see page 287)* $ _____

Detail Plan Packages: *(see page 287)*
- ☐ Framing ☐ Electrical ☐ Plumbing $ _____

  SUBTOTAL $ _____

Sales Tax - MO residents add 6% $ _____
- ☐ Shipping / Handling *(see chart at right)* $ _____

  TOTAL ENCLOSED *(US funds only)* $ _____

I hereby authorize HDA, Inc. to charge this purchase to my credit card account (check one):

☐ MasterCard   ☐ VISA   ☐ DISCOVER NOVUS   ☐ AMERICAN EXPRESS Cards   ☐ LOWE'S

Credit Card number _____

Expiration date _____

Signature _____

Name _____
(Please print or type)

Street Address _____
(Please do not use PO Box)

City _____

State _____   Zip _____

Daytime phone number (____) - _____

I'm a ☐ Builder/Contractor   I ☐ have
- ☐ Homeowner   ☐ have not
- ☐ Renter   selected my general contractor

Thank you for your order!
288

Important Information To Know Before You Order

- **Exchange Policies -** Since blueprints are printed in response to your order, we cannot honor requests for refunds. However, if for some reason you find that the plan you have purchased does not meet your requirements, you may exchange that plan for another plan in our collection within 90 days of purchase. At the time of the exchange, you will be charged a processing fee of 25% of your original plan package price, plus the difference in price between the plan packages (if applicable) and the cost to ship the new plans to you.

  Please note: Reproducible drawings can only be exchanged if the package is unopened.

- **Building Codes & Requirements -** At the time the construction drawings were prepared, every effort was made to ensure that these plans and specifications meet nationally recognized codes. Our plans conform to most national building codes. Because building codes vary from area to area, some drawing modifications and/or the assistance of a professional designer or architect may be necessary to comply with your local codes or to accommodate specific building site conditions. We advise you to consult with your local building official for information regarding codes governing your area.

Questions? Call Our Customer Service Number
314-770-2228

Blueprint Price Schedule   *BEST VALUE*

Price Code	1-Set*	SAVE $110 5-Sets	SAVE $200 8-Sets	Reproducible Masters
AAA	$225	$295	$340	$440
AA	$325	$395	$440	$540
A	$385	$455	$500	$600
B	$445	$515	$560	$660
C	$500	$570	$615	$715
D	$560	$630	$675	$775
E	$620	$690	$735	$835
F	$675	$745	$790	$890
G	$765	$835	$880	$980
H	$890	$960	$1005	$1105

Plan prices guaranteed through June 30, 2006.
Please note that plans are not refundable.

- **Additional Sets* -** Additional sets of the plan ordered are available for $45.00 each. Five-set, eight-set, and reproducible packages offer considerable savings.

- **Mirror Reverse Plans* -** Available for an additional $15.00 per set, these plans are simply a mirror image of the original drawings causing the dimensions and lettering to read backwards. Therefore, when ordering mirror reverse plans, you must purchase at least one set of right-reading plans. Some of our plans are offered mirror reverse right-reading. This means the plan, lettering and dimensions are flipped but read correctly. To purchase a mirror reverse right-reading set, the cost is an additional $150.00. See the Home Plans Index on pages 286-287 for availability.

- **One-Set Study Package* -** We offer a one-set plan package so you can study your home in detail. This one set is considered a study set and is marked "not for construction." It is a copyright violation to reproduce blueprints.

*Available only within 90 days after purchase of plan package or reproducible masters of same plan.

Shipping & Handling Charges

U.S. SHIPPING - (AK and HI - express only)	1-4 Sets	5-7 Sets	8 Sets or Reproducibles
Regular (allow 7-10 business days)	$15.00	$17.50	$25.00
Priority (allow 3-5 business days)	$25.00	$30.00	$35.00
Express* (allow 1-2 business days)	$35.00	$40.00	$45.00

CANADA SHIPPING (to/from) - Plans with suffix 032D or 62D	1-4 Sets	5-7 Sets	8 Sets or Reproducibles
Standard (allow 8-12 business days)	$25.00	$30.00	$35.00
Express* (allow 3-5 business days)	$40.00	$40.00	$45.00

Overseas Shipping/International - Call, fax, or e-mail (plans@hdainc.com) for shipping costs.
* For express delivery please call us by 11:00 a.m. Monday-Friday CST